The
Weimaraner

An Owner's Guide To

A HAPPY HEALTHY PET

Howell Book House

IDG Books Worldwide, Inc.
An International Data Group Company
Foster City, CA • Chicago, IL • Indianapolis, IN • New York, NY

Howell Book House
IDG Books Worldwide, Inc.
An International Data Group Company
919 E. Hillsdale Boulevard
Suite 400
Foster City, CA 94404

For general information on IDG Books Worldwide's books in the U.S., please call our
Consumer Customer Service department at 800-762-2974. For reseller information,
including discounts and premium sales, please call our Reseller Customer Service
department at 800-434-3422.

Library of Congress Cataloging-in-Publication Data
Riley, Patricia.
The Weimaraner/Patricia Riley.
    p. cm.–(An owner's guide to a happy healthy pet)
Includes bibliographical references.
ISBN 1-58245-171-0
1. Weimaraner (Dog breed) I. Title. II. Series.
SF419.W33R56   2000
636.752–dc21   00-038888

Manufactured in the United States of America
10 9 8 7 6 5 4 3 2 1

Series Director: Susanna Thomas
Book Design by Michele Laseau
Cover Design by Iris Jeromnimon
External Features Illustration by Shelley Norris
Other Illustrations by Jeff Yesh
Photography:
    All photography by Mary Bloom unless otherwise noted.
    Joan Balzarini: 96
    Mary Bloom: 96, 136, 145
    Paulette Braun/Pets by Paulette: 96
    Buckinghambill American Cocker Spaniels: 148
    Sian Cox: 134
    Dr. Ian Dunbar: 98, 101, 103, 111, 116–117, 122, 123, 127
    Dan Lyons: 96
    Cathy Merrithew: 129
    Liz Palika: 133
    Susan Rezy: 96–97
    Judith Strom: 96, 107, 110, 128, 130, 135, 137, 139, 140, 144, 149, 150
Production Team: M. Faunette Johnston, Angel Perez, and Heather Pope

Contents

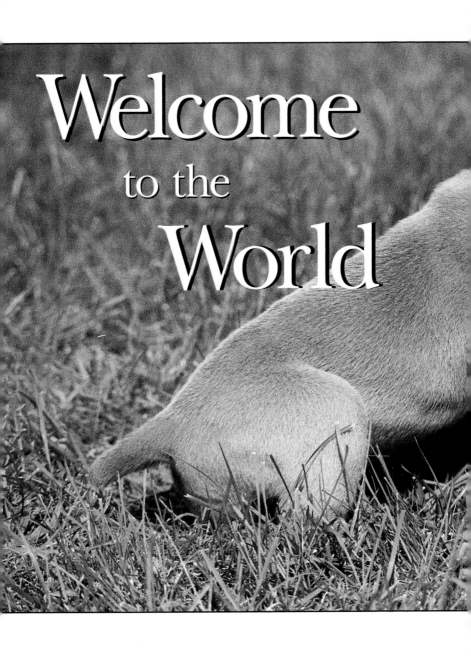

Welcome
to the
World

of the
Weimaraner

External Features of the Weimaraner

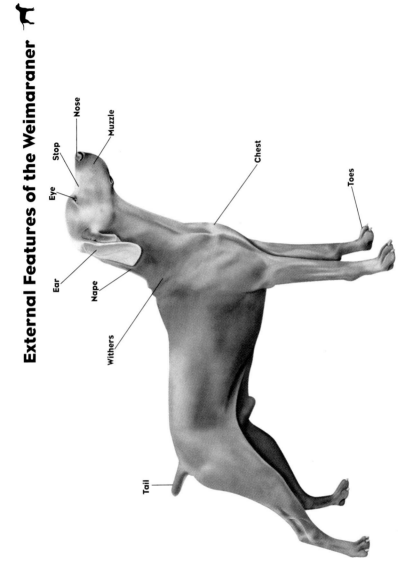

chapter 1

What
Is a
Weimaraner?

The first thing that comes to mind when people think of a Weimaraner is "that silver dog with the amber eyes." With those words you have begun the description of the Weimaraner. But it is only the beginning—loyal companion, energetic playmate, tireless hunting partner are also words that come to mind. The Weimaraners' remarkable coloration and haunting eyes make them a stand out almost anywhere they may go; their friendly attitude and intelligence make them as popular as

they are striking in appearance. A Weimaraner is more than a medium-size gray dog; he is an attitude, and a lifestyle.

A Versatile Dog

In the United States, Weimaraners have served in many capacities. Their versatility is literally legendary. Serving as companions or hunting partners is but a small portion of the vast repertoire of the Weimaraner. They have served in police departments and the military as protection, rescue, and detection dogs. Documentation even shows a Weimaraner served as a guide dog for the blind. Primarily used by hunters as upland bird dogs in the United States, historically, in their native country of Germany, they are also used to track large, wounded game of all sorts including boar, bear, and stag, tracking and retrieving smaller game, such as rabbits. Today Weimaraners participate in a staggering array of activities from those recognized by the AKC to less common ones such as weight pulls, ski-joring, Frisbee, flyball, and more.

Both athletic and intelligent, Weimaraners are are happiest being a part of a family with an active lifestyle.

A dog that is athletic and intelligent, the Weimaraner can be an ideal family companion. Of medium to large size and high activity level, they are dogs best suited to families with active lifestyles. The Weimaraner is not a dog that will tolerate languishing in a kennel or yard, but demands, loudly and actively sometimes, to be a part of the family. Their short, easy-care coat shrugs off water, burrs and dirt, and requires only minimal grooming to maintain their appearance, complementing the lifestyle to which they would like to become accustomed—part of your life, that is. Easy to train and eager to please, Weimaraners quickly learn to adapt to whatever activities you and your family enjoy. While friendly under most circumstances, they are devoted to their family and can become protective of their people and property.

The Breed Standard

When discussing the perfect Weimaraner it is important to remember that the dog described in the standard approved by the American Kennel Club is theoretical. And while every Weimaraner should *look* like a Weimaraner, if your dog doesn't meet the ideal of the standard, he can still be a valued family member and a great companion. The purpose of the standard is to identify the features unique or identifying to the breed, and to provide a basis on which to judge and compare Weimaraners at a conformation show. You can get a copy of the American breed standard from the American Kennel Club. Most aspects of the standard serve to maintain the breed's usefulness in relation to its historic purpose. Unless you are interested in competing in conformation shows or breeding, deviations from the standard are only important in how they affect your dog's health and participation in your life.

> **WHAT IS A BREED STANDARD?**
>
> A Breed Standard—a detailed description of an individual breed—is meant to portray the ideal specimen of that breed. This includes ideal structure, temperament, gait, type—all aspects of the dog. Because the Standard describes an ideal specimen, it isn't based on any particular dog. It is a concept against which judges compare actual dogs and breeders strive to produce dogs. At a dog show, the dog that wins is the one that comes closest, in the judges' opinion, to the Standard for its breed. Breed Standards are written by the breed parent clubs, the national organizations formed to oversee the well-being of the breed. They are voted on and approved by the members of the parent clubs.

GENERAL APPEARANCE

"A medium-sized gray dog, with fine aristocratic features. He should present a picture of grace, speed, stamina, alertness and balance."

It is almost impossible not to recognize a Weimaraner at first sight. Their balanced body type is moderate in all things, lacking extremes in any feature, except their aristocratic mien. Aristocratic does not mean soft or weak though: Every aspect of the Weimaraner should indicate their suitability for working long hours in the field.

SIZE

The Weimaraner is considered a medium-sized dog. Males should be 25–27 inches tall at the withers and females 23–25 inches tall. There is a great deal of variation in size in different bloodlines. Males can be as tall as 30 inches and females as short as 20 inches. However, a dog that is smaller or larger than the desired height by more than 1 inch either way would be disqualified from a con-

Weimaraners don't have to measure up to every aspect of the breed standard to make a loving and loyal pet.

formation show. Weight may range from 45 pounds to over 100 pounds. The size of the ideal Weimaraner keeps in mind the breed's historic uses. A very small dog was not able to cover large expanses of territory while hunting, or to be able to face down large game as easily as a larger dog. An overly large dog was cumbersome to transport, subject to stress injuries and often actually slower in the field than a more moderate size dog.

THE HEAD

"Moderately long and aristocratic, with a moderate stop and slight median line extending back over the forehead."

Again that aristocratic appearance! And the word "moderate"—twice! A correct Weimaraner head would never be confused with the heaviness of a Mastiff head, the blockiness of a Labrador head, or the fineness of an Afghan head. For the Weimaraner, the distance from the tip of the nose to the stop (where the muzzle joins the skull) should be equal to the distance from the stop to the occipital bone (where the top of the skull joins the neck), giving a balanced appearance. The stop should be obvious but not contribute to a squareness of the skull, but rather slope back into the skull. The median line is a slight indentation that runs from the stop to the top of the skull. In puppies the occipital bone is normally very prominent but tends to moderate with maturity.

The neck of the Weimaraner should lend a balanced look to the dog. A short, thick neck is a more common fault than one that is too long. The proportion of the head and neck contribute to the appearance and physical balance of a dog in motion—and Weimaraners are usually in motion.

The American Kennel Club standard describes the Weimaraner's head as "aristocratic."

EYES

When you get your Weimaraner puppy his eyes will probably be the most beautiful shade of blue you have ever seen in a dog. Take lots of pictures; as your puppy begins to grow up the blue will usually fade and then change to yellow and often darken to amber. Sometimes the color will be different in each eye. Occasionally a dog will keep his blue eyes, though not the typically brilliant blue of a puppy. There is no evidence that eye color affects the dog's visual acuity. The acceptable eye colors for Weimaraners are light amber, gray, or blue gray.

EARS

Because of their size and high set (placement of the ears on the skull), the Weimaraner's ears contribute a great deal to their expressive face, from a forward alert

position, or laid tightly back against the skull expressing embarrassment, submission, or coyness. The ears are large, and rather long, but not pendulous or hound-like. When held snugly alongside the dog's head the ears should end about (but not more than) 2 inches from the tip of the nose. The fur on the ears is typically softer and finer, and sometimes a lighter color, than on other parts of the body. The ear leather itself frequently has folds and curves that are typical and a hallmark of the breed. It is also common for the edges to thicken as the dog matures. In puppies the ears are very large in proportion to the rest of the head, but like all their excess skin on their little bodies, they usually grow into them.

Take a long look now, because your puppy's pretty blue eyes will likely change to amber before you know it.

TEETH

Teeth are important to any hunting breed, and are not typically a problem in Weimaraners. In fact, their canine teeth are relatively larger than in many breeds. To be effective as a retriever and defender the teeth should be strong and well set in the jaw, and meet in a scissors bite. That means that there should not be more than $1/16$ of an inch between the top incisors and the bottom incisors when the dog's mouth is closed (if you can easily slide the tip of your fingernail there, it is probably more than $\frac{1}{16}$ of an inch). The flesh inside the mouth is normally a pink (gums) to a pinkish gray (inside lips and palate) color, sometimes with liver-colored mottling.

BODY

Primarily a hunting dog, the Weimaraner's body should again reflect his ability to work in the field. Just because he is a gentleman, does not mean that he is not an athlete. Moderation is the keyword. A correct back should be strong and tight (but not inflexible) when the dog moves at a trot. Although there is a moderate amount of slope to the topline (where the spine runs from the withers to the hips) when the dog is standing still, when the dog moves, the topline will remain relatively level. The back should not be so long as to cause strain on the vertebrae or muscles. This would be apparent as excessive flexing in the spine when the dog moves at a trot. A back that is too short does not allow the dog to take advantage of his full stride and he either interferes with himself when moving, or he moves with a short, choppy, inefficient stride.

Even if you don't plan on hunting with your Weimaraner, these relationships within your dog's physique can still affect his ability to interact with you. If you expect your Weimaraner to go jogging, hiking or compete in any type of athletic activities, these factors can affect your dog's ability to perform, both in the short-term and long-term.

THE AMERICAN KENNEL CLUB

Familiarly referred to as "the AKC," the American Kennel Club is a nonprofit organization devoted to the advancement of purebred dogs. The AKC maintains a registry of recognized breeds and adopts and enforces rules for dog events including shows, obedience trials, field trials, hunting tests, lure coursing, herding, earthdog trials, agility and the Canine Good Citizen program. It is a club of clubs, established in 1884 and composed, today, of more than 500 autonomous dog clubs throughout the United States. Each club is represented by a delegate; the delegates make up the legislative body of the AKC, voting on rules and electing directors. The American Kennel Club maintains the Stud Book, the record of every dog ever registered with the AKC, and publishes a variety of materials on purebred dogs, including a monthly magazine, books and numerous educational pamphlets. For more information, contact the AKC at the address listed in Chapter 13, "Resources," and look for the names of their publications in Chapter 12, "Recommended Reading."

TAIL

The tail is another distinguishing characteristic of the Weimaraner. While many breeds have their tails docked, the Weimraner's is typically longer than most. At maturity the tail should be about 6 inches long and cover the genitals. If it is docked too short, there's not much you can do. Some owner's have had tails re-docked if they are too long, but there is really not much reason to unless you are competing in conformation events; and even then, the carriage of the tail may be permanently affected. The original docking is done at the same time the dewclaws are removed.

Even though a Weimaraner's tail is docked, it is not as short as in many other breeds. The veterinarian docks the tail while your dog is still a puppy.

COAT AND COLOR

"Short, smooth, and sleek, solid color, in shades of mouse-gray to silver-gray, usually blending to lighter shades on the head and ears."

Probably the most distinguishing feature of the Weimaraner is his color and coat. As your Weimaraner matures, you will notice changes in the shading over his body. A lighter "cap" on the back of the head is common, as are the ears being much lighter than the body color. It is also common, and no cause for alarm, for the tail to be almost white in a younger dog. This is most likely the result of the docking procedure, and it will fade with age to match the rest of the body. When a Weimaraner approaches his annual shedding, his coat may develop a speckled appearance.

An unusual variation of coat color is the "blue" Weimaraner. The blue color is a disqualification in the conformation ring, but does not indicate that a dog is not purebred. It is not always obvious at first glance to tell whether a dog is blue or gray because some of the gray dogs may be a shade so dark as to appear almost blue, and some blues are so light as to appear gray. Genetically, gray dogs have a base color of brown and blue dogs have a base color of black. The primary clue is in the pigmentation of skin, particularly around the eyes, mouth and the nails. In the blue Weimaraner this pigment will typically be very dark—almost black; in a gray dog the nails will be gray or amber, and the pigment around the eyes will be light.

Weimaraners are known for their lustrous, wash-and-wear coats.

Another color variation is tan or "dobe" markings. This variation is linked to the complicated genetic combination that results in the distinctive gray coat of the Weimaraner. Again, it does not indicate, all by itself, that your Weimaraner is not purebred. In fact, the

13

subject is not even addressed in the breed standard other than the requirement of a "solid color."

Another, more frequent variation, is the long coat. These dogs are at least as striking in appearance as their short-coated brethren. The long-coated variation is recognized as acceptable in conformation competition in almost all countries except the United States. A source of considerable controversy in the United States, the long coat varies from a Brittany type to a thicker, longer coat similar to a Golden Retriever.

The Weimaraner is not the kind of dog who likes to be alone. She needs lots of socialization.

TEMPERAMENT

In this day and age, any discussion of dogs would be incomplete without also including temperament. The standard calls for a dog that is "friendly, fearless, alert, and obedient." While it is true that most Weimaraners do have wonderful temperament, it is not *only* the result of good breeding. As a responsible Weimaraner owner *you* must be proactive. Weimaraners are strong, intelligent, active dogs. Without direction they will become strong, intelligent, active, destructive nuisances. Weimaraners need you to give them constructive outlets for their energy. A Weimaraner who spends many hours separated from his family, or without activity can be incredibly destructive.

Another issue for Weimaraner owners is socialization of their dogs. Without plenty of exposure to life outside the home, including people, dogs and activities, Weimaraners can become insecure or overly protective. It is *essential* that you get your puppy out in the world in a responsible, constructive manner. Remember, the Weimaraner evolved not only as a hunting dog, but also as a defender, so you should expect a Weimaraner to bark and alert you when strangers are near, or become protective. It is up to you to teach your Weimaraner what is acceptable and responsible protective behavior.

Also plan on teaching your Weimaraner basic obedience. Obedience classes are a great place to meet other folks interested in their dogs, as well as getting the basic tools to control your dog in many different types of situations. Kindergarten puppy classes are often available now, and they are great fun for you and your puppy as well as educational. Refer to Dr. Ian Dunbar's books which can provide information on choosing classes for your puppy or adult dog (see Chapter 8). Observe the instructor teaching several classes and different levels of classes to be sure you are comfortable with the way the classes are run, and the methods and techniques used. Weimaraners are intelligent, eager-to-please dogs that will respond well to training that focuses on positive, motivational techniques.

Taking a basic obedience class together will bolster the relationship you and your Weimaraner share.

chapter 2

The Weimaraner's Ancestry

For many years it has been traditional to accept that the Weimaraner was developed by Carl Augustus of Germany in the late 1700 to early 1800's. More recent research by Debbie Andrews and Jackie Isabell has produced convincing evidence tracing the origins of the breed as far back as the court of Louis IX in the 13th century! Isabell and Andrews have outlined the fascinating evolution of the breed from the *Chien Gris de Saint Louis* (Gray Hound of Saint Louis) through the courts of royalty throughout Europe in their book, *Weimaraner Ways.* Pictures and written descriptions of the Chien Gris de Saint Louis bear a striking resemblance to the Weimaraner.

In the late 1700's and early 1800's this type of dog was "stabilized" as a breed and brought to prominence by Carl Augustus of Weimar.

The dog's German name *der Weimaraner Vorstehund* translates as "pointing dog of Weimar." The breed was highly prized as a hunting dog of German royalty with strict requirements to be met before being permitted

to own one. Good secrets are hard to keep and, although fiercely preserved as a hunting dog of the aristocracy, as time went by the breed spread across Europe, gaining an equal reputation not only as a highly qualified hunting companion but as the "Forester's Dog" as well. The Weimaraner could not only find, track, and retrieve game, but also defend the forest manager from poachers and game.

The first standard for the breed was published in 1894 amidst considerable controversy because some officials believed it to be simply a variation of the German Shorthaired Pointer breed standard. The first Weimaraner breed club was established in 1897 and developed strict membership requirements, as well as testing and breeding protocols.

Throughout history, royalty and commoners alike have prized Weimaraners for their hunting and tracking abilities.

The Weimaraner Comes to the United States

The first known Weimaraners imported to the United States arrived in 1929 with Howard Knight. The Weimaraner Club of America held its first meeting in 1943. The American Kennel Club granted official recognition of the breed that same year. But it was not until after the conclusion of World War II that Americans became familiar with the breed. With scarce resources and strict regulations regarding hunting and ownership of firearms, many Europeans sold their dogs to U.S. soldiers. According to some sources, in addition to his well-known bull terrier, Patton also owned a Weimaraner, which accompanied him across Europe. As a result of stories printed about the Weimaraner in the early 1950's the popularity of the breed caught fire. The stories told about the Weimaraner's prowess in the field that required little to no training, unbelievable stamina, and incredible intelligence. Weimaraners were prominently featured in advertising as well. President Dwight Eisenhower, Roy Rogers, and Grace Kelly are but a few of the well-known Weimaraner owners of the time. As the breed's popularity soared, demand predictably increased. And just as predictably, more people began breeding more puppies. Thought was not always given to the quality of the puppies produced, and as a result, the outstanding qualities of the breed were undermined. Additionally, many new Weimaraner owners had unrealistic expectations as a result of the build up of the "Wunderhund."

By the 1960s the popularity of the breed began to decline. After the indiscriminate breeding frenzy of the 1950s to meet public demand, the breed developed a reputation for a lack of mental and physical soundness. This reputation decreased the breed's popularity and provided responsible breeders with the opportunity to begin to rebuilding the breed. Even now, however, some professional trainers would rather not have these intelligent, easily trained dogs in their classes because of the reputation they developed in the '60s.

THE PHOTOGENIC WEIMARANER

In the 1980s Weimaraner popularity began to rise again as the work of the well-known photographer and artist William Wegman gained recognition. Wegman's first work with Man Ray, *Man's Best Friend*, was published in 1982. Man Ray was followed by Fay Ray, and later her puppies Battina, Crookie, Chundo, and others. These Weimaraners are photographed in a vast array of unlikely postures, positions, and poses that appeal not only to our aesthetic sense, but to our sense of humor as well. In the 1990s Wegman began publishing series of children's books covering the ABCs, shapes, fairy tales, and more. Fay Ray was a frequent guest on the children's show Sesame Street, helping children to learn their ABCs and to count. Two of Mr. Wegman's recent works include *Puppies*, a photo-biography of Fay Ray's litter, and *Fay*, a touching tribute.

Once again Weimaraners are becoming popular because of their use in advertising. My own dogs have appeared in commercials, and are frequently requested to be photographed. There is something amazingly photogenic about Weimaraners at any age or any circumstance.

The Heritage of the Modern Weimaraner

Although not the most common dog used in bird-hunting, the Weimaraner's history has established her as the "gentleman's gun dog," not just suited to the hunter on foot, but for nearly any style of hunting.

The heritage of the dogs of early Europe, as defenders of their masters as well as hunting dogs, lives on in the Weimaraner of today. Although all Weimaraners need training to become good citizens, their instincts of right and wrong, safe and dangerous, are well developed.

American servicemen brought Weimaraners home to the United States following World War II. (above) Weimaraners have earned the status of "Gentleman's Gun Dog." (left)

Owning such a dog is a great responsibility; it requires an owner who is willing to respect the heritage and instincts of the breed, and provide socializing and sensible training to develop a confident and responsible companion. While generally a well-behaved, congenial breed, and a pleasure to own, you need to guide your Weimaraner in a clear understanding of what her responsibilities and limits are. It is not too difficult to teach her what you expect, but left to her own devices, any Weimaraner will make her own rules.

19

chapter 3

The **World** **According** to the **Weimaraner**

Welcome to the world of the Weimaraner. In this new place you will never be bored and never be alone. Everything is interesting, exciting and meant to be shared, from dinner to your shower. The Weimaraner wants to be a part of your life, and he will insist upon it as his natural right. Not a dog that is content to languish in the back yard, he will loudly tell your neighbors of his unhappiness, he will share it with your garden as he excavates, and take it out on the garden tools you left outside. On the other hand, a tired Weimaraner is a happy Weimaraner. Take him with you on your daily jog (after physical maturity), family camping trips, and the weekly softball games. He will gladly accompany you, help carry equipment and shag those long flies. With proper training, a Weimaraner is a gracious family member, loyal, dutiful and responsible. He is not a dog suited to every person or circumstance; he has been bred to be an active hunting dog, expected to use his brains and all his senses. Although many people get a Weimaraner as a companion, these old instincts must be acknowledged.

At Home

Plan on getting your Weimaraner out and active at least once a day, for at least an hour. Brisk walks, games of fetch, Frisbee, jogging, he won't care as long as he can be with you. Fail to provide the physical activity for him and he will start looking for his own! Most Weimaraners will be happiest sleeping next to your bed—in your bed given even half an invitation. Don't be surprised if your Weimaraner protests at being left outside, or in the back room when it is time to settle down for the night. His heritage gives him the responsibility and privilege to protect you while you sleep.

Generally a fairly robust breed, Weimaraners do not have much subcutaneous fat or a thick coat to protect them from cold weather—some lack a good undercoat to protect them from wet conditions. So dry, comfortable quarters in colder or wet conditions are a must. The Weimaraners' generally clean, neat habits, make them wonderful housedogs, despite their size.

House privileges are not something Weimaraners take lightly either. All of my dogs have shown an amazing ability, despite their active, sometimes frenetic, playtimes to avoid plowing into people, walls, furniture or breakables. And, they have learned housetraining very quickly. More than once they have shown an acute sense of embarrassment when a moment's lack of

An active Weimaraner is a happy Weimaraner.

*Their short
coats, clean
habits and
protective
instincts make
Weimaraners
ideal housedogs.*

self-control resulted in bumping into the coffee table or a puddle on the floor. The flipside is that when someone rings the door bell, the meter man comes, or the kids get too rowdy, they are just as likely to take action; depending on training, with anything from a bark or two to a full scale 100 decibel barking barrage.

Obedience training is a must with Weimaraners. Unless you explain to them how you want them to co-exist with you, they will set their own rules. So start early and be consistent. Most Weimaraners will do best in classes that focus on positive motivation, such as clicker training.

Emotional Needs

Socialization is an important aspect of raising a Weimaraner. A Weimaraner has a strong instinct to protect what he views as his. By getting your young puppy out and letting him see that the world is a fun, friendly place, full of nice people with lots of good things to eat and play with, you will be well on the road to a happy well-adjusted adult Weimaraner. Make it a point to get your puppy out every day during his first 6 months of life and let every man, woman, and child you meet pet and feed your puppy. Pet first, then feed.

(Hint: Only allowing your puppy to accept food when he is sitting will go a long way toward teaching him not to jump on people, too.) This intense socialization will wear off if it is not consistently repeated, so be sure to get your dog out and about in the world on a regular basis. Dogs that are poorly trained are often left home because of their unruly or undesirable behavior. A dog that is lacking in proper socialization becomes more upset or agitated in unfamiliar surroundings and it becomes a vicious circle. Jean Donaldson's book *Culture Clash* and Shelia Booth's *Purely Positive Training* have some excellent tips on socializing a dog that are well suited to the Weimaraner.

The current literature about separation anxiety in dogs says that it manifests itself as uncontrollable excessive behavior in the absence of the owner beyond what would be considered normal. Where a bored dog may bark excessively, or chew, a dog suffering from separation anxiety may work himself into a frenzy. The barking takes on an entirely different, desperate tone, the chewing is compulsive and may even include self-mutilation, such as excessive licking (often on the forelegs) or tail chewing. If you think your dog may be suffering from separation anxiety, consult your veterinarian. Although new treatments exist for this problem, which include medication as well as behavioral modification, it is much better to avoid the situation altogether.

Socializing your puppy now will ensure that she is a pleasant-to-be-around adult later.

Start to teach your Weimaraner from a young age that being alone is okay. If your pup seems particularly upset by your absence, teach him first that it is okay to be in a separate room, and progress from there. Be sure to make leaving a low-key event.

Things to Do

Remember the Weimaraner's history? That's right—breeders originally bred Weimaraners as hunting dogs! Most Weimaraners *love* to hunt. If you go for walks, they will be trailing rabbits, pointing squirrels, and flushing songbirds. Several organizations provide wonderful opportunities to hunt with your dog and earn titles and prizes. The American Kennel Club offers not only field trials for the competitive at heart, but hunting titles for those who just want to prove their dog can do it. Additionally the Weimaraner Club of America has rating tests which require only one passing score. And then the National Association of Versatile Hunting Dogs offers the most comprehensive, owner friendly test, starting with the Natural Aptitude Test and going up to the Utility Test.

If you teach your puppy that it is okay to be alone, he won't experience serious separation anxiety. He will always miss you when you are gone, but he won't work himself into a frenzy waiting for your return if you train him correctly.

If you are not into hunting you can still test your dog's nose in tracking tests. Training a Weimaraner to track is a lot like teaching a bird to fly. Sandy Ganz and Susan Boyd have an excellent book *Tracking From the Ground Up*.

Looking for more social activities? Well, Weimaraners are flashy competitors in the obedience ring. And with positive training methods their enthusiasm and team-work are a spectacle to behold! While Weimaraners are virtual slaves to their noses, with consistent, positive training, a Weimaraner will give his all for you. And all those exercises are not only useful in the competition ring, but are endlessly handy at home, too. Want your dog to wait while you open the car door? Come back to you after he has been playing in the park? Walk politely on a leash? All of these skills are basic exercises in competition obedience! At the more advanced levels the Weimaraner's natural skills come into play: jumping, retrieving and scent discrimination.

Tracking is an activity that your Weimaraner will jump into with all fours! (top) Their athletic form and innate intelligence make Weimaraners naturals at agility competition. (left)

Looking for something a little more free form? Weimaraners and agility go together like milk and cookies! These dogs are natural athletes and love the thrill of running, jumping, climbing, and burrowing. In fact, the hardest part of training a Weimaraner in agility is teaching him to pay attention to the details, like waiting at the start line, hitting the contact zones, and taking direction. If you think you are interested in dog agility, just go watch an agility trial. It won't be long before you are hooked.

Do you want to do something to benefit your community? With proper training Weimaraners have served as both Search-and-Rescue dogs and Therapy dogs. The training is demanding, intense and time consuming. Missions can be emotional roller coasters of highs and lows. Handlers and dogs are required to re-certify on a regular basis to maintain their mission-ready status.

Therapy dogs serve in a variety of ways. Some visit the elderly in nursing homes, others offer cheer to hospitalized children and still others visit children who have been victims of trauma, abuse, or neglect. Once again, there is a lot of training involved and a process of certification and re-certification on a regular basis. It also requires a long-term commitment of a portion of your time, usually on a weekly or monthly basis. See Chapter 13, "Resources" for books on these subjects.

It is important to keep in mind that the Weimaraner was bred to use his brain and all of his senses. Any training needs to take these facts into account. Use his heritage to your benefit. For example, if you are interested in competitive obedience and want to teach your dog to keep his attention focused on you,

---

A DOG'S SENSES

Sight: With their eyes located farther apart than ours, dogs can detect movement at a greater distance than we can, but they can't see as well up close. They can also see better in less light, but can't distinguish many colors.

Sound: Dogs can hear about four times better than we can, and they can hear high-pitched sounds especially well. Their ancestors, the wolves, howled to let other wolves know where they were; our dogs do the same, but they have a wider range of vocalizations, including barks, whimpers, moans and whines.

Smell: A dog's nose is his greatest sensory organ. His sense of smell is so great he can follow a trail that's weeks old, detect odors diluted to one-millionth the concentration we'd need to notice them and even sniff out a person under water!

Taste: Dogs have fewer taste buds than we do, so they're more likely to try anything—and usually do, which is why it's especially important for their owners to monitor their food intake. Dogs are omnivores, which means they eat meat as well as vegetable matter like grasses and weeds.

Touch: Dogs are social animals and love to be petted, groomed and played with.

keep a small toy (such as a kong or ball) hidden in your hand. As a reward for remaining focused for one second toss the toy for your dog to chase. Gradually increase the amount of time you expect your dog to remain focused. Before long your Weimaraner will reward you with a penetrating gaze as he waits and watches intensely for you to release his prize.

Additionally, in comparison to some breeds, the Weimaraner is slow to mature, both physically and mentally. This is easy to forget when your young dog is so willing and learns so many skills so quickly. If you are expecting your Weimaraner to go out his first season and point steady to wing and shot, honor, and retrieve to hand, your expectations may be too high for the average Weimaraner. Although many do a credible job in their first season, they are often impulsive. Give your dog time and sensible training for whatever you expect him to do and he will remember it for a very long time. Combined with their desire to be part of your life you will find your gangly, impulsive puppy will finally mature into the loyal, capable companion you desire.

With enough training, you and your dog can get involved in community service in a variety of ways.

The Versatile Breed

Recognizing the heritage of the breed, the Weimaraner Club of America offers a Versatility program. Dogs earn the Versatile or Versatile Excellent title by earning points for titles in various activities. It is not the least bit unusual to see a Weimaraner with titles in conformation, hunting, obedience, tracking *and* agility. And all these activities are not just fun; they keep your Weimaraner physically and mentally active—an essential for keeping you and your Weimaraner happy.

27

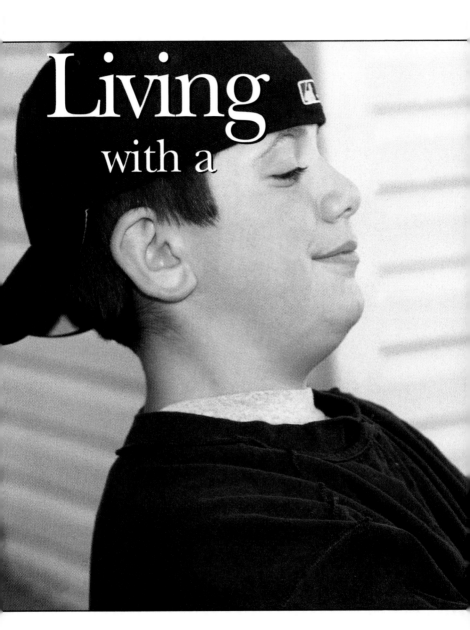

Living
with a

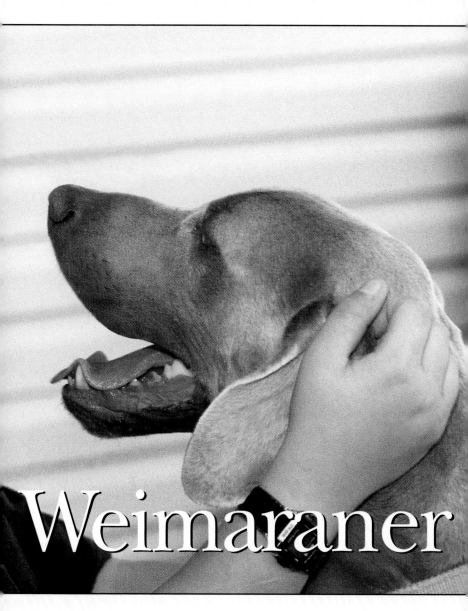

part two

Weimaraner

chapter 4

Bringing
Your **Weimaraner**
Home

If you have already chosen your puppy, welcome to the Weimaraner world! If you haven't selected your puppy yet, be sure to read as much as you can about the breed and talk to as many Weimaraner owners as you can to get to know the breed before you bring a puppy home. Dog shows, obedience, agility, and field trials are great opportunities to see these dogs and meet their owners. When you are looking for a Weimaraner puppy, remember that you are making a 13- to 17-year commitment, so choose wisely.

Finding a Puppy

If you choose to get your puppy from a breeder, keep in mind that a good breeder will have almost as many questions for you as you have for them. They have invested a lot of time and money into their litter and they want to be sure the puppies are going to appropriate, loving homes. It is not unusual for a responsible breeder to request that you to sign a contract. The contract may specify certain conditions that you will have to meet, such as providing a fenced yard, allowing the dog to live in the house or follow a particular vaccination protocol.

Some indicators of the responsibility of the breeder are as follows. First, is there a buy-back clause? In the event that you decide you are unable to keep your Weimaraner, a truly responsible breeder will want first shot at getting the dog back so he or she can be sure the dog is placed in a responsible home.

Another thing to look for is a guarantee. A responsible breeder will guarantee the basic health and certain genetic aspects of your puppy. Most offer some sort of compensation or exchange if the puppy does not work out in this respect. Every breeder should offer you a timeframe to take your new puppy in for a veterinary exam after your take your puppy home. Along with guarantees, you may often see certain health certifications on the parents. Some health problems in dogs, such as hip and elbow displaysia, thyroid problems, and certain heart problems, are believed to be strongly influenced by genetics.

Finding a trustworthy source for your new Weimaraner is the first step towards bringing your adorable puppy home.

A breeder should test for problems common in their breed and offer these registry ratings and numbers when you inquire about puppies. Requesting to see a copy of the certificates identifying the parent dogs and their ratings is entirely acceptable. Fortunately, in Weimaraners, not too many health problems remain hidden throughout puppyhood.

Finally, a responsible breeder should be involved in other Weimaraner activities besides just breeding puppies. They should be constantly pursuing additional education in the many aspects of raising dogs, including genetics, nutrition, training and general health. They should be promoting ethical and responsible breeding practices, as well as the physical, mental, and genetic soundness of the breed. Keep in mind, it is not snobbish to look for titles from the parents of your puppy. After all, these titles indicate an investment of time and money by the breeder to determine the worthiness of a dog to be in a breeding program. Additionally the titles indicate a degree of trainability and temperament in the dogs earning those titles. Hopefully they will pass those qualities on to their offspring.

PUPPY ESSENTIALS

Your new puppy will need the following items:

food bowl

water bowl

collar

leash

ID tag

bed

crate

toys

grooming supplies

A few final clues are the age at which the breeder releases the puppies, the age of sire and dam, and how many litters the breeder produces at a time, or in a year. A puppy should *never* be released prior to 6 weeks of age. Research shows that 7–8 weeks is even better. Most people are not prepared to cope with the special needs of a puppy younger than 6 weeks old. Besides, those weeks before a puppy goes home with her new family are critical to her emotional development. A puppy learns how to interact with other dogs and people during this time. Removing her too early may not give her the opportunity to learn important lessons from her mother and littermates.

If you get your puppy from a breeder, it is important that you feel comfortable with the breeder you select.

After all, you will share a common bond for many years to come! A breeder is a terrific source of information for you, with many years of experience in dog psychology, training, and health. You may find yourself calling with questions about surviving your puppy's first night home, housetraining, nutrition, obedience training and more.If you are selecting your own puppy from a litter, be sure to listen to what the breeder has to tell you about the individual puppies. Every puppy is an individual, and not every puppy in a litter will be right for your home. Some puppies will be very bold and outgoing; they may be too much for an inexperienced dog owner, or a home with very small children. A very shy puppy will require a very experienced owner to ensure that it does not develop into a fearful adult. From the breeder's perspective, the most promising pup in the litter would ideally go to a prospective show- or field-competition home.

If you get to meet your puppy's litter, it is a good sign if all pups look healthy and happy.

All the puppies should be clean and look healthy. Their eyes and noses should be free of any discharge. Their coats should be clean and shiny. While they should not be fat butterballs, they should not look emaciated either. The environment that the puppies are living in should be spotless; it should look and smell clean. Fresh water should always be available. Often you will see a variety of toys available to stimulate the puppies' mental development: chew toys, plush toys, maybe even a box or tunnel to play in. Puppies should be friendly and gregarious, as should the parents. If possible, meet both parents of the litter, their personality and temperament will give you many clues to what the future holds for your puppy!

Are You Ready?

Now the moment is at hand! Your new puppy will be coming home soon. Are you ready? Are you sure? One of the first things you will want to do is take your puppy to visit the vet. Have you selected one yet? Be sure to read through Chapter 7, "Keeping Your Weimaraner Healthy," for tips on selecting the right veterinarian. Long before your puppy comes home, stop and take a look around. The first thing to do is make sure you have all the "necessities." Your puppy will need all sorts of things to get through the day and night. Most everything you need can be purchased at a pet supply store or through a pet supply catalog. Catalogs are usually a great source for getting the best prices, but if you aren't sure what you want, then head to the pet supply store so you can see what all the options are and try things out.

BOWLS

Does your pup need her own food and water bowls? Of course. More than one? Yes. When your puppy comes home she will probably be eating three meals a day. Food bowls *must* be washed after each meal. Food crumbs remain no matter how thoroughly your pup scours the bowl. Would you eat breakfast off a plate and then use it again for lunch without washing it first? So, unless you want to wash after each meal, get more than one bowl. I really like quality stainless-steel bowls. Dogs rarely chew them, they don't break, and they can be washed in the dishwasher. Ceramic dishes come in a huge assortment of really cute designs and can be washed easily, but they also break fairly easily and some made outside the United States are decorated with lead based paints!

Plastic dishes are easily chewed and the pits and grooves from chewing and scratching can become sharp. If you cleaned your plate with your tongue you would have a good idea why this can be an important issue. Those pits and grooves are also hard to clean. Aluminum dishes can leach the metal into food and often aren't as durable. Besides, for the price, you can't beat the durability and safety of stainless steel.

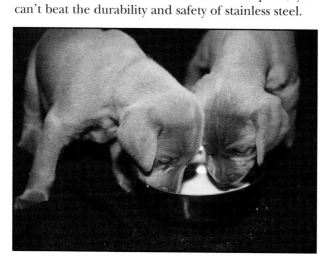

Stainless-steel bowls are the best value for your puppy.

FOOD

You should actively discuss the type and brands of food you should feed your puppy with your breeder, other Weimaraner owners and your veterinarian. Also, read through Chapter 5, "Feeding Your Weimaraner," before you go out and buy that first bag of food. If your puppy comes from a breeder, he or she will probably send some puppy food home with you, so you won't need to buy any food immediately.

BEDS

Your puppy will also need a bed. Besides saving wear and tear on furniture and carpet, a dog bed defines a specific space that your puppy can go to and be comfortable, out of the way and still be able to see what is going on in the household. The bed should definitely be washable. An old blanket folded up will work fine, but there are lots of different options in the pet supply market today. Round, rectangular, donut, or ball shaped, they may be stuffed with Holofil™ or cedar and polyfill. Some are made with foam stuffing. If you buy a ready-made bed, be sure that the outer liner can be removed and washed. Buy an extra cover for your convenience at laundry time. Remember, puppies will chew on anything, so check the condition of the bed frequently to make sure your pup doesn't have access to the filling.

CRATES

A crate can be a double-edged sword. When used properly it is the best way in the world to keep your puppy safe and happy when you can't be there to supervise. Of course, if you leave your pup confined in an

improperly sized crate for hours on end, it is cruel, plain and simple. But when properly used, it is an indispensable tool in raising your puppy. The two biggest advantages of having a crate, and teaching your puppy to love it, are when you are traveling and when you are housetraining.

When you first bring your puppy home you will need to teach her when and where to urinate and defecate.

Used properly, a Weimaraner's crate becomes her personal escape from the world.

A crate makes this process a thousand times easier for *both* of you. Your puppy's instincts will tell her not to soil her "den." So she will try to wait until you let her out of her a crate. If she should have an accident in the crate, it is easier to thoroughly clean and disinfect than your carpet. Housetraining will be covered in depth a little later.

If your puppy was shipped to you, she probably came with a puppy-sized crate that will last for a month or two until she outgrows it. After your pup outgrows her baby-sized crate, you can move her on into her adult-sized one, by then she will have the basic idea.

Having a crate gives your puppy a space that is unequivocally hers. Although she should always allow you entrance to any space, a crate gives your dog a place to go when she wants to be alone, or escape the hustle and bustle of family life.

Crates can be either plastic "airline" type, or wire mesh. Each has its advantages. For most people the plastic type will probably be most useful because if you ever ship your dog, that is the kind you will need anyway. Just be sure to check the bolts on a regular basis, as they have a tendency to come loose even if the crate is never moved. Such small loose objects are sure to attract the attention of a curious Weimaraner puppy, and they are definitely not good for her to chew or swallow. The plastic crates come apart for storage, and the wire variety usually folds flat.

EXERCISE PENS

Exercise pens are a handy, but not vital item. Think of them as a puppy playpen. If you are gone for extended hours during the day, the exercise pen gives your older puppy a little more room to move around. They are also handy in the yard if you want to limit the area your puppy has access to. When traveling they are a real help in letting your puppy have some play time without worrying about whether or not the hotel room or friend's home is puppy proof.

> ### HOUSEHOLD DANGERS
>
> Curious puppies and inquisitive dogs get into trouble not because they are bad, but simply because they want to investigate the world around them. It's our job to protect our dogs from harmful substances, like the following:
>
> #### IN THE GARAGE
>
> antifreeze
>
> garden supplies, like snail and slug bait, pesticides, fertilizers and mouse and rat poisons
>
> #### IN THE HOUSE
>
> cleaners, especially pine oil
>
> perfumes, colognes and aftershaves
>
> medications and vitamins
>
> office and craft supplies
>
> electric cords
>
> chicken and turkey bones
>
> chocolate and onions
>
> some house and garden plants, like ivy, oleander and poinsettia

37

Using a baby gate is an easy way to limit the access your Weimaraner has to your home.

Baby Gates

You won't want to give your puppy free reign of the house until she won't chew on inappropriate items and she has shown that she can consistently let you know when she needs to go out. The solution in the meantime is the baby gate. They come in a wide variety of materials and sizes. Some can even be mounted permanently, and swing open with a latch! Baby gates are a great way to protect the rest of your house while your puppy is learning the rules and they will save you a lot of headaches and clean up. Best of all they can be moved to give access to larger areas as your puppy learns to be more responsible, and they can be taken down when guests come, or other times when the puppy is confined in an exercise pen or a crate.

Leash and Collar

If your puppy was shipped, she probably will come without a collar (for safety reasons), so you will need to have one when you pick your puppy up. There is an incredible selection of collars available, in thousands of colors and designs. Keep in mind that your puppy will be pretty small when you get her—it seems obvious, but lots of people end up with a collar big enough for the puppy to climb through! My first choice is the very soft braided nylon type. They are infinitely adjustable because the tongue of the buckle just goes right through the fabric, and puppies seem to become accustomed to them most quickly. Choke-type collars, either fabric or metal, are not appropriate for puppies and must not ever be left on any dog of any age when they are unattended due to the possibility of strangulation.

Leashes can be of matching material, but I personally prefer leather leashes. They are easier on the hands

and will last almost forever as long as you don't leave
them were your dog can find them and chew on them.
If you decide to make a fashion statement, fabric
leashes are available in an incredible array of colors
and styles. When you are looking at leashes remember
that your puppy is just a little baby, so buy a lightweight
leash to start with, braided nylon (matching the collar)
makes a great first leash. As an adult you will probably
want a $^3/_8$-inch to $^1/_2$-inch fabric or leather leash with a
quality snap.

Pooper Scooper

Another handy item for the modern-day dog owner is
the pooper scooper. Since you should be picking up
daily after your dog, this item will save a lot of wear and
tear on your back. And because it is more convenient
than a regular shovel, you will be more willing to pick
up more often, which is better for your dog. There are
several types available. Some come with a small bag
attached to a long handled scoop. (I have never found
this type easy to use, but some folks swear by them.)
The most practical and economical scooper comes in a
two-piece set. One piece is a metal tray attached to a
long handle for holding the feces. The other piece is a
long handled rake or spade. I personally prefer the
rake, but to each his own; the spade type is easier to
find. Although ideally you would pick up as soon as
your dog deposits, this rake or spade/tray arrange-
ment is convenient if you only pick up once a day, or
are picking up after several dogs. Remember to clean
the tray and rake on a regular basis.

Toys!

This is where it really gets fun! There are literally thousands of dog toys on the market these days. But
restrain yourself. There is no consumer advocate
group out there to make sure that the toys are safe.
And from a training aspect, if your puppy has 100 different toys to play with, it makes it pretty hard for that
little puppy brain to figure out which are toys for her
and which ones are not. So pick out two or three to

begin with. Make sure they are durable. Remember those baby puppy teeth evolved to be able to tear and chew meat off the bones of prey. They will easily dissect the cute stuffed toys, as well as many vinyl toys—and those squeakers can result in big vet bills if they are swallowed. Weimaraners can be very aggressive chewers so be sure to keep an eye on your puppy or adult dog when introducing a new toy.

Other good chewing toy purchases are marrow or shank bones—good, solid, beef bones at least two inches long (four to six inches long is ideal for adult dogs). Fresh or frozen, dogs adore chewing the meat off of them and later they can be stuffed with peanut butter and frozen just like the Kong toy. Even a Weimaraner can spend an hour or more getting the last smudges of peanut butter from the middle of a

bone. The most important thing to remember about bones is that they are generally safe as long as they are large enough and *raw*. Cooked bones tend to splinter.

Weimaraners, for the most part, love to play fetch games, and Frisbees are a great way to exercise your Weimaraner. Just be aware that the ones manufactured for human use are easily chewed up and can be hard on

Toys provide great outlets for all the chewing your puppy longs to do.

your dog's teeth and gums. There are a couple of versions available that have been created with dogs in mind. My favorite is the Floppy Disk, it is made of nylon fabric that floats, flies, and can be washed when it gets dirty. It is also easier for most dogs to catch. New models have a rope around the edge and are only partially covered with canvas. This type is more durable if your dog enjoys a vigorous game of tug also. Best of all, these can be crunched up in your pocket when you are done. The Floppy Disk is probably a toy more suitable for a dog beyond the puppy age, when the desire to chew everything has passed. Balls and retrieving bumpers are great for fetch, but aren't really good choices for unsupervised play. The fuzzy cover can be torn off and swallowed and bumpers can simply be dissected. But keep several on hand, because Weimaraners really do love to play fetch.

Rawhide chews, and similar products like pig ears and cow hooves, are a controversial subject. Most dogs love these products. However, once you have stepped on a half chewed rawhide in the middle of the night, you will probably throw them all out. But the greatest controversy lies in the possibility of intestinal blockage or choking. It is possible for a dog to chew off a large enough chunk to either lodge in the throat or in the intestine. Either of these situations is potentially fatal. If you do choose to allow these products for your dog, do so only under supervision, and if you are feeding pig ears or cow hooves be sure to take their nutritional value into account when feeding since these are high in protein. Also be very careful in selecting your chew toys. Some, particularly those produced outside the United States, are processed with potentially dangerous chemicals. Once again, there is no consumer advocate to monitor the safety of dog products.

Plush toys and puppies look cute together, but be sure to supervise your puppy while she has one. Your Weimaraner puppy may be able to chew some of the parts off of the toy and swallow them, a dangerous practice!

Plush toys are everyone's favorite. Puppies look *so* cute carrying them around. They also often like to curl up and sleep with plush toys creating a great photo opportunity for a few hundred pictures to send relatives and friends. However, the plush toy is another example of a toy that is not suitable for unsupervised play. These are too easy to dissect; button eyes, squeakers, and stuffing can result in major vet bills. So if you can't resist them, give them to your puppy only when you can monitor the chewing. Choose safe toys, inspect them often, and replace them when necessary.

THEY'RE ALL CHEW TOYS

Now get down at puppy level and look around. See that hanging extension cord? Looks like a chew toy to a puppy. The fact is, nearly everything is a chew toy to a puppy. So select a room with a floor that is easy to clean, put up your puppy gate and start putting away anything that isn't necessary. Save yourself the heartache, and put Aunt Betsy's afghan in another room for a while, along with the crystal, and anything else you would be distressed to have chewed or broken.

Household plants deserve a special discussion. They seem to be particularly attractive to puppies. Unfortunately, many can be poisonous. Not only for your puppy's safety, but also to reduce the likelihood of developing a bad habit, remove all houseplants *far* out of your puppy's reach. If you leave plants in the room, make sure they are non-poisonous and out of reach.

Electrical cords and curtain ropes are other special hazards. Both are very satisfying for puppies to chew on, and potentially very hazardous. Cords can not only cause severe shocks when chewed on, but like curtain ropes, electrical cords can also wrap around a puppy, either the neck or another body part, and cause serious injury. Many curtain cords now come with special "breakaway" balls to prevent strangulation, but unfortunately, puppies see these as potential toys and can swallow them whole or crunch them into dangerously sharp pieces that can be swallowed. A clothespin can temporarily keep curtain ropes out of reach, and special tacks from the hardware store can secure necessary electrical cords along baseboards where they are less tempting.

DEODORIZER

Don't forget some disinfectant and deodorizer. Your puppy is bound to have a few accidents. When the inevitable puddle appears, you need to clean it up so thoroughly that your puppy's sense of smell will not lead her back to the same spot. Her nose is much sharper than yours so don't depend on your sense of smell. Purchase products from a pet supply catalog or store that are designed to both disinfect *and* deodorize dog urine and feces. Be sure to test the products in a hidden spot first!

Grooming Supplies

Weimaraners don't need extensive grooming, but you will need a brush or a grooming glove, nail clippers, and a few other supplies. Read through Chapter 6, "Grooming Your Weimaraner," before you browse the catalogs or make your trip to the pet supply shop.

Identification

Another important item to consider is permanent identification for your dog. Of course you will get identification tags for your dog's collar. But collars can slip off. What happens if you are on vacation and your dog gets lost? There are now a couple of choices for permanent identification for your pet.

One choice, in addition to collar tags, is a tattoo. Your dog's registration number can be permanently inked onto your dog. The most favored site for a tattoo is inside the thigh of the hind leg. The process is fast, permanent, and not terribly uncomfortable for your dog. A tattoo on a Weimaraner is easily seen, and AKC registration numbers are easily recognizable as such. Don't use your phone number or address as these may be subject to change, confusing and useless for someone who finds your dog. The problem with tattoos is that they may fade or stretch over time.

Technology has provided a more recent option, the microchip. The microchip is a rice-sized capsule injected under your dog's skin, usually between the shoulder blades. The microchip gives off a signal that can be picked up by a special scanner. The scanner reads the microchip's unique number. The microchip number is usually registered with a national organization and/or your county dog regulatory agency.

If you make sure your Weimaraner has proper identfication at all times, chances are better that you will be reunited should he ever get lost.

Your best bet is the shotgun approach: chip, tattoo and collar identification. Be sure to take pictures of your puppy as she grows so that you will always have a good picture to use for flyers if necessary. Family pictures are cute, but be sure you get some good side and front facing pictures that will provide identification for someone who is not familiar with the breed or your dog as an individual; all Weimaraners look alike to someone who doesn't own one. Also write down identifying features of your dog, like the small white spot behind the pastern, or the scar on his shoulder, a chipped tooth, anything that will help unequivocally identify *your* dog to a stranger.

Who Is That Puppy?

Selecting a name for your puppy is probably one of the most fun things about getting a new dog. Naming a dog is an extremely personal experience but here are a few suggestions to help you and your dog survive the experience. While there is certainly nothing wrong with more traditional names, if you want something more contemporary, there are many books available for selecting a name for your dog. Don't be afraid to check them out. Some offer names specifically for German dogs, if you prefer something in line with your dog's German heritage.

Keep in mind your dog's personality, heritage, and physical characteristics when you choose a name. Don't forget your own dignity! If you aren't comfortable calling "Precious" at home, what will you do when you are at the park? Also keep in mind your dog's limitations. If you call out "Maximillian of Silver Bells" across the park, it is not likely your dog will realize that this string of sounds is actually supposed to mean him. If you have a registered dog, it is fine to send that in as the official name, but as far as your dog is concerned, "Max" is a better choice.

Start using your dog's new name as soon as possible. Use it often, but use it with meaning. Don't just call out her name without some action following it, or she will learn to tune it out! "Echo! Dinnertime!" "Friday! Walk?" "Keya! Get that toy!" Try to associate the name with something good and your puppy will soon turn her head when you call her. When she does recognize her name, make sure something good happens. If you call your puppy's name and she responds by looking at you, praise her immediately and walk over and give her a treat. In no time at all your puppy will learn to focus on you whenever you call her name, a *very* useful habit.

Choose a name for your puppy that you feel best matches her personality.

Where Is That Puppy?

Did you buy that crate? Whether or not your puppy sleeps on the bed with you is a personal decision, but be forewarned, once you do it the first time, it is *really* hard to explain to your dog later that the rules have changed. We put a puppy's crate in our bedroom to help keep puppy safe while we sleep. The key to teaching your dog to settle down in a crate is to start out putting her in it for a short time at first and *never* opening the door when she is not quiet. Stand firm. Your puppy won't yelp forever—at the very least she has to breathe sometime.

The first time you introduce your puppy to the crate put a few treats inside and let her investigate them and the crate. Start using a word for going into the crate right away; show your puppy the treat, toss in the treat, give your command. After a few tries, your puppy should go in and out with no worries. Then you can close the door for just a second so your puppy will realize there *is* a door. As soon as puppy stops, usually with a puzzled look, but before she has the opportunity to complain, praise her and then open the door. Praising and opening the door rewards the puppy for being quiet. *Slowly* increase the amount of time you leave the door closed. Usually over the course of a day you can work up to several minutes.

It is best to decide in advance where that adorable new puppy is going to sleep. Once he gets a taste of your bed, you may have a furry bedfellow for life.

The exception to this rule is at night. Puppy will have to be confined to her crate during the night, and you can't possibly work your puppy up to eight hours or so of confinement on your first day together. But if you have introduced her to the crate during the day, it will minimize her frustration and complaints that night. Save a very special (quiet) toy to give to your puppy only at night in the crate. Remember: Opening the crate door while your puppy is fussing reinforces the behavior and increases the likelihood of the behavior being repeated. It doesn't take long for a dog to figure out that if she screams and yells, you will let her out. Just like a child's temper tantrum in the candy aisle, give in once, and you pay for it over and over.

Housetraining

One of the biggest problems puppy owners complain about is housetraining. For most puppies, housetraining is really not difficult. The number one rule of housetraining is that if your puppy has an accident, it is *your* fault. Use that rolled up newspaper on yourself, not your puppy! A schedule, a leash, and a crate are the keys to success in housetraining. Take your puppy, on the leash, out to the spot you prefer her to use. When your puppy is very young, carry her, but graduate to walking on a leash as soon as possible. Plant your feet in one spot, and give your chosen command ("go potty," "get busy," "hurry up" are common) just as you see your puppy squat. Quietly praise your puppy, and when she is finished give her a small treat, and some play. It is important to remain in one place while your puppy is searching for "the right spot." Many a dog has learned that the longer she takes to go the longer you stay out there with her. By remaining in one place, it quickly becomes boring. It is not enough to send your puppy into the yard by herself, you will have no idea whether she urinated or not!

If your dog defecates outside your property *always* clean it up with the plastic bags you *always* carry when you take your dog out. It is your responsibility as a dog owner to clean up after your dog, so don't leave it for someone else. Picking up after your dog is polite and considerate, and in some places, it is the law. No one wants to step in what your dog left behind. I don't mind cleaning up after my dogs, but it sure ticks me off to have to clean up after someone else's. Not everyone likes dogs; leaving "landmines" is more ammunition for anti-dog legislation.

If your puppy has just emptied her bladder, then you probably have about a half an hour of safe playtime. If puppy has an accident immediately after you bring her in, then you need to give her more time to go outside.

47

If puppy didn't urinate, then put her back in the crate for a little while and try again. Every time your puppy gets it right, you have made one more step toward getting your puppy housetrained. If you see your puppy squatting to urinate or defecate inside, a sharp "No!" and hand clap, will often startle her into "holding on." Scoop up your puppy and leash and head to the usual spot. No scolding! The "No!" is only to startle, not to punish. Your puppy really doesn't know she is not supposed to urinate in the house. So, give her plenty of chances to learn.

Your puppy is likely to need to relieve herself after waking up and eating. Some puppies will also benefit from the opportunity to relieve themselves after playing. Most puppies will warn you by circling and/or sniffing. Many quickly learn to head toward the door used to go to the "right" spot. At a minimum, give your puppy the chance to relieve herself every two to three hours and definitely as the last thing you do before bedtime. And remember, just because your puppy has gotten it right for several days does not mean your puppy is housetrained—just that you have been diligent. Soon you will see your puppy head for the door when she needs to go out. Tell her what a good dog she is and take her right out. Watch for this behavior and praise it at every opportunity.

A TYPICAL HOUSETRAINING SCHEDULE

Wake up; take puppy out immediately (puppy will most likely urinate)

Feed puppy and take him back out (puppy may urinate, will likely defecate)

Playtime!

Naptime

Immediately when puppy wakes go outside.

Mealtime

Go outside

Playtime

Naptime

Go outside

Playtime

Mealtime

Go outside

Playtime

Go outside right before bedtime

It is not hard to teach a puppy to ring a bell to ask to go out. Unless it is an "emergency exit," smear a tiny bit of peanut butter on, or wiggle your fingers behind a bell hanging at puppy level, right next to the door you use to go outside to the designated potty spot. As soon as puppy noses it, whether it rings or not, praise and exit. She'll get the idea quickly.

If your puppy seems to urinate frequently, or if you have been consistent and vigilant and your puppy is still having accidents, discuss the possibility of a urinary tract or bladder infection with your veterinarian.

Welcome Home

It is exciting to get a new puppy. And you are probably eager to show off your fuzzy new family member to your friends and relatives. After all, puppies are about the cutest thing around. But please give your puppy a few days to settle in and get accustomed to all the new surroundings before you have everyone over to see your adorable bundle of fur.

Be proactive in watching out for your puppy. Painful or scary things that happen to your young puppy can make a real impression and affect how your puppy responds even as an adult. Be very choosy about letting adult dogs play with your young puppy. Be sure they won't intimidate or hurt your puppy. And insist that any dog or puppy be healthy and current on vaccinations.

It's okay to be picky about your puppy's playmates at first. Children may not know how to correctly handle the puppy, and other dogs may be unpredictable or not vaccinated.

Not everyone knows how to handle or behave around a puppy. Be ready, for example, to intervene if small children try to pick up your puppy. Don't allow your puppy to jump up to greet people even at this

49

young age. It will become a habit all too quickly, and a 75-pound Weimaraner putting his paws on your chest and licking your face is not everyone's idea of fun. So ask guests to come all the way into the house first and then squat down to greet the puppy without letting the puppy put her paws on them. Limit guests to one or two at a time if possible so as not to overwhelm the puppy with too much noise and excitement at one time. With that said, it is a great idea to have people over to meet your puppy often from the time she is young until she is well past 6 months old and frequently even as an adult. This will help prevent your adult Weimaraner from developing a sense of territoriality, and minimize barking and anxiety when guests come over.

Are You Sure?

Before you bring a new puppy home, be honest and look at your schedule and lifestyle. Young puppies really need the opportunity to relieve themselves during the day. Will there be someone who can let the puppy out *at least* once during the day? Will someone need to come home from work to do so? Or can you take the puppy to work with you? Puppies need exercise too. If you and your family come home at night and want to just collapse on the couch, will you really want to take the puppy for a walk and some playtime? Can you stand a few nights without a full night's sleep? Are you willing to invest the time and money into the necessary obedience training? Answer these questions honestly *before* you bring your puppy home.

Older Dogs

Raising a puppy involves a huge investment of your time. Maybe you want a dog, but just don't have as much time as is needed for a puppy. Consider adopting an older dog. Each year dogs lose their homes due to a variety of reasons, divorce, death of an owner, a new baby, new home, or new job. A few are rescued from abuse or neglect. Some of these dogs have special needs; others just need a new family. Contact the Weimaraner Club of America for a contact in your area if you are interested in offering your home to one of these special dogs. But be prepared to face a scrutinizing adoption procedure, at least as stiff as any breeder placing puppies. The placement organization makes

every effort to match the personality of a dog with the appropriate family to ensure a permanent placement.

When bringing an adult dog into your home, much of the previous information still applies. Be sure to give the dog time to become accustomed to her new home and family with as little stress as possible. Don't schedule a vacation or a party around the time your dog arrives. After the initial settling in period, plan on enrolling your new dog in a basic obedience class using strong motivational training, even if she already has some training. The class will foster the bonding process between

you and your dog and help establish structure and rules in an unfamiliar situation. It also gives a new owner the chance to offer frequent praise and positive input. Weimaraners often become very attached to "their" people so be patient and understanding as your dog comes to terms with her changed circumstances. It won't be long before you are "her people."

Sometimes adopting an older dog is the best alternative. Older dogs are usually house-trained, and will bond to you soon enough.

chapter 5

Feeding
Your
Weimaraner

What you decide to feed your Weimaraner is probably one of the most important decisions you will make for your dog. It can also be one of the most overwhelming decisions because of the choice of types of food and the many brands. Probably the two overriding factors in choosing what food to feed your dog are the affect the food has on your dog's health and the cost. The two are closely related; if you buy a cheap food, you may end up paying more in veterinary bills. Conversely, just because a food is expensive doesn't mean it is the best for your dog. Liz Palika's book *The Consumer's Guide to Dog Food* will give you a basic education on how foods are manufactured and just what you are getting. She also includes a questionnaire to help

you decide on the type of diet that satisfies your needs
as well as your dog's.

Types of Commercial Foods

Commercial dog foods can be broken down into three
basic categories: dry, semi-moist, and canned. Canned
foods are generally the most expensive and space consuming to store. They are expensive because their
water content creates a larger volume and the difficulty
in maintaining their freshness. The biggest advantage
to canned foods is that most dogs will eagerly wolf
them down. The disadvantages of canned foods are the
expense and possible connection to periodontal disease. Canned foods may be appropriate if your dog is
extremely active, or has a high metabolism and you
need to encourage him to eat larger volumes than he
otherwise might.

Semi-moist foods often come wrapped in individual
servings, and are exactly what the name implies. The
advantage of these types of foods is their high palata-
bility. Most dogs will eagerly eat almost any semi-moist
food, just as a child might eagerly eat a candy bar for
breakfast every morning. However, that doesn't mean
that either food is nutritious. The disadvantage of
these foods is their questionable nutritional value and
expense. They are frequently processed with a great
number and variety of artificial colors, flavors, and
preservatives, as well as an excessive amount of sugar
products.

Dry foods, or kibble, are probably the most economical for the large-dog owner. An educated shopper can
find a nutritious, affordable food for his Weimaraner
on the shelves of kibble at the local pet supply shop.
Remember, when you are reading labels, that dogs
evolved as carnivores; so a meat-based diet, supplemented with small amounts of vegetable matter is most
likely to satisfy his nutritional needs. It is extremely difficult to provide a balanced vegetarian diet for dogs.
Meat, not meat by-products, should be, at a minimum,
one of the first three ingredients.

Quality ingredients probably won't be the least expensive. Although cost is not the most definitive way to determine the quality of ingredients, it is one sign. Let's face it, if the manufacturers are charging rock bottom prices, they can't be buying the best quality ingredients.

Another important factor to consider is the number of preservatives and artificial additives. Many artificial colors have been linked to health problems in the past. Some are still used in pet foods, although they have been prohibited from use for human consumption. The colorings are added for your benefit (the paying customer) not the dog's (the actual consumer). If your dog doesn't care what it looks like, why should you? Pass by the artificial colorings whenever possible.

There is a possibility the preservatives BHA, BHT and ethoxyquin may be linked to cancer and liver damage, among other problems. Currently long-term tests are being conducted to test these possibilities. Due to this increasing concern, more foods are now available on the market that advertise themselves as organic and/or preservative free or naturally preserved (most often with Vitamins C and E or tocopherols). A label from one such brand includes turkey, chicken, (first and second ingredients!) apples, potatoes, rice, alfalfa sprouts, and more. Sounds pretty yummy! Take the time to research a little into your dog's food options; after all, it is in the interest of your dog's health.

HOW TO READ THE DOG FOOD LABEL

How can you be sure you are feeding the right food to your dog? The information is all there on the label—if you know what you're looking for.

Look for the nutritional claim right at the top. Is the food "100 percent nutritionally complete"? If so, it's for nearly all life stages; "growth and maintenance" is for early development. Puppy foods and foods for senior dogs are specially marked so you can choose the proper food for your dog's stage.

Ingredients are listed in descending order by weight. The first three or four ingredients will tell you the bulk of what the food contains. Look for the highest-quality ingredients, like meats and grains, to be among them.

The Guaranteed Analysis tells you what levels of protein, fat, fiber and moisture are in the food, in that order. Although these numbers are meaningful, they won't tell you much about the quality of the food. The nutritional value is in the dry matter, not the moisture content.

In many ways, seeing is believing. If your dog has bright eyes, a shiny coat, a good appetite and a good energy level, chances are his diet's fine. Your dog's breeder and your veterinarian are good sources of advice if you're still not sure which food is appropriate.

Life Stage Foods

Today's market also offers many specialized types of foods for the different life stages of your dog: puppies, active dogs, overweight dogs, or older dogs. Puppy foods tend to be a little more nutritionally dense since puppies can't eat as much food at one time. They also tend to be higher in protein and fat than regular foods. The appropriate age to change to an adult food varies greatly with the individual dog since some dogs will mature much later than others. As a general rule, your Weimaraner can probably be switched to adult food sometime after 9 months and definitely by 18 months of age. Look for signs that your dog has reached physical maturity when deciding if your dog needs to change to an adult food formulation.

Offering your Weimaraner the right food will help him stay beautiful and energetic.

If your dog is used for hunting, competition or participates in other physically demanding activities, you may want to consider a performance food. Again, these tend to be more nutritionally dense and higher in protein to meet the dog's greater physical demands. They often contain a higher fat content as well. It is very important if your activity is seasonal, such as hunting, that you monitor your dog's condition after the season, and either reduce the volume you feed, or switch back to a regular diet.

Formulas for overweight dogs are usually lower in protein and fat and higher in fiber than regular foods. For most overweight dogs the answer is more often simply reducing the volume fed or increasing the activity level. Read the section on weight control later in this chapter.

Some new foods for older dogs contain special nutritional supplements (discussed in the supplementation

section) to ease the aging process as well as being lower
in fat and protein. The affect of the level of protein in
older dogs is still subject to debate. Dogs with compro-
mised kidney function will definitely benefit from
lower protein levels and higher protein quality.
Although every Weimaraner will age at a different rate,
your Weimaraner is typically considered a senior after
the age of 8. If you switch to a food for older dogs, be
sure to monitor your dog's weight and response to the
new food. Discuss your dog's nutritional needs with
your veterinarian if you think that the food you are
feeding is not appropriate for your dog.

*Some owners
choose to make
their own dog
food, which
dogs generally
gobble up with
gusto.*

Home Cooking for Canines?

An increasingly popular option is the "whole food" or
"natural" diet. Each year more books are coming out
about this feeding option. *Dr. Robert Pitcairn's Complete
Guide to Natural Health for Dogs and Cats* is considered a
classic in this field, and a good starting point; Wendy
Volhard's *Holistic Guide for a Healthy Dog* is an excellent
companion as well. At this point in time, there is no
definitive research showing that nutritionally balanced
natural diets are any better, or worse, for your dog.
Many people find that they enjoy the feeling it gives
them to prepare homemade diets for their dogs.

People who have been feeding this type of diet for an extended time will swear by the improved health and appearance of their dogs. Others will tell you of the disappearance of chronic health problems such as allergies, and improvements in skin and coat, whelping, orthopedic and behavioral issues, even reduced tartar. Many will tell you that their dogs actually have a better diet and are healthier than they are themselves.

How Often?

How often to feed your Weimaraner is a function of your dog's age and your schedule. Young puppies cannot properly digest large volumes of food at one time, so meals must be fed more frequently. A puppy between 2 and 4 months of age will likely be eating three times a day, spaced as evenly as possible throughout the day. Your puppy will likely begin to show a disinterest in the mid-day meal and let you know when he is ready to switch to twice a day. After that, twice a day feeding will contribute to your dog's overall health and improve his digestion. If you are feeding a whole food diet you may be able to feed your mature dog once a day.

Weimaraners are rarely finicky eaters. Those that are have usually schooled their owners into catering to this behavior rather than naturally being picky. Avoid falling into this trap. Any healthy dog that is being offered nutritious food will eat when he gets hungry.

If your dog is turning up his nose at what you offer, ask yourself a few questions: Is this a food my dog has normally been eating? Is it a new bag? Always check the packaging code to be sure you are getting a fresh bag. If the store employees can't show you how to read the date on a particular brand, call the company; they will be happy to tell you. By shopping at a store with high turnover you can get fresher food. Examine the bag for signs of spoilage, such as greasy stains, or evidence of pests. If your dog becomes ill after opening a new bag, call the toll-free number on the bag and talk to the company. New bag or old, smell it. Does it smell "off"? Could household chemicals possibly have contaminated an opened bag? How is your dog's weight? Maybe your dog is telling you he is getting too much food. How about those between meal snacks? Just how many dog biscuits is your dog getting between meals? Check with everyone in the family! Does your dog look like he is feeling poorly? Trust your instincts, often your sub-conscious is speaking to you. You see your dog everyday; you know what is normal. For most of my dogs, skipping one meal causes me to keep a sharper eye on that dog. Skipping two meals almost always results in a trip to the vet. Weimaraners just don't like to be hungry.

Once in a while, your Weimaraner may not eat what you offer him. One skipped meal is nothing to worry about, but two skipped meals in a row may warrant a trip to the veterinarian.

If your dog doesn't clean up the bowl in fifteen minutes, remove the bowl. You don't want to encourage snacking; it is much more difficult to monitor the eating habits of a snacker. Leaving food out encourages the growth of potentially harmful bacteria, contamination, and spoilage, even with dry foods.

How Much?

Dog food companies are in the business of selling dog food. The more your dog eats the more bags of food they sell. Feeding trials are most often conducted with Labradors and Beagles, two breeds that in general have different metabolisms than Weimaraners. So read recommendations on the bag with a skeptical eye, use them as a starting point. The average Weimaraner generally eats less what the bag suggests. Let your dog tell you how much is the right amount. If your adult Weimaraner's back has a distinctly broad appearance, if he lacks a visible waistline when viewed from above, if there is more than a thin layer of fat at the base of the tail, if the ribs can not be easily felt through a thin layer of fat, and if your dog lacks a distinct tuck behind the ribs, then you probably need to reduce your dog's caloric intake. If, on the other hand, your Weimaraner has a distinctly bony appearance, the ribs are visible or easily felt under the skin, and the tuck behind the ribs and waistline are extreme, then you should probably increase your dog's calories.

Remember that your dog's caloric needs change as he passes through puppyhood, and even as a mature dog. Even the changing of the seasons can trigger a change. It is not unusual for young adults, particularly males, to have a sudden rapid increase in their metabolism. It usually will settle back down after a few weeks. The point is that you need to monitor your dog's physical condition on a regular basis.

HOW MUCH IS TOO MUCH?

If, after taking a good, honest look at your Weimaraner, you have decided that perhaps he is carrying a bit too much weight, why does it matter? First and foremost, just like people, those excess pounds are hard on your dog's health. Not only on things like his heart, kidneys, and liver, but on bones, joints, and muscles too. Overweight dogs are more prone to injuries as well as illness. Also, because most Weimaraners enjoy being active, those excess pounds make that harder to do too.

So, what are you going to do? The first thing to do is determine how much your dog is really eating. Find out who is feeding him, how often and how much. I knew one couple that figured out that both of them were feeding the dog dinner! Don't forget to add in all the snacks and treats. Most commercial dog treats are high in empty calories. Just reducing the number of snacks and increasing the amount of exercise can often be the solution. If your dog is excessively over-weight, reducing snacks isn't working, or you have other health concerns, consult your veterinarian.

Take into account all snacks and treats when measuring out your dog's food. An overweight Weimaraner doesn't have the freedom to enjoy life the way a healthy Weimaraner does.

Snacks and Treats

In one respect, dogs are very similar to people: They enjoy a good snack as much as we do. And just like people, the wrong kind of snack can be bad for them. Sweet, sugary snacks are worse for your dog than they are for you. A dog's metabolism just didn't evolve to handle those types of foods. In particular chocolate is actually toxic to dogs. A surprisingly small amount can cause serious and immediate health problems. Unfortunately, many dogs seems to love it as much as any human chocoholic, so don't leave it where your dog can even possibly get to it. At our house chocolate either goes in the refrigerator or on the top shelf of a pantry with a door catch. Friends and family know better than to send gift-wrapped food items, especially chocolate.

If you read the labels of many dog snacks, you will find sugar products as a major ingredient in many of them. While reading, mentally include all the sugars on the ingredient panel (there are many different types) in one group—you'll see how much sugar there really is. By listing each type of sugar separately, the manufacturer's hope you won't notice that some of those snacks are as much as 15 percent sugar! If you choose to feed commercial snacks, avoid those with multiple types of sugar, or where sugar is a major ingredient (one of the top five). Also, be aware that many commercial snacks contain artificial colors and preservatives.

When you feed your dog treats and snacks remember to keep in mind that those snacks contain lots of calories, just like people junk food. If your dog is getting a little on the pudgy side, either cut back on the snacks or find healthier alternatives. Believe it or not, dogs really like lots of other things! Some favorites of my dogs: raisins, Cheerios, granola (can be high in fat), cheese, grapes, popcorn (unbuttered, unsalted), carrots, frozen green beans, homemade jerky, dehydrated or fresh fruit, frozen fruit juice and ice cubes. There are several books available on making healthy homemade snacks for your dog if you are the culinary type.

Unless you are careful to establish boundaries for your Weimaraner, you may be playing tug-o-war with your steak dinner next time!

Table Manners

Weimaraners can not only be inveterate beggars, they can quickly learn to be first-rate thieves! Unless you enjoy having a steak disappear off your plate between bites, establish mealtime manners early. We have always taught our dogs to "leave the kitchen" when a meal is on the table. They are free to watch, quietly, but from a respectable distance. Their eyes are usually glued to the scene, memorizing the drop of every crumb, but they are not allowed back in until the table is cleared. Using an easily identified marker, such as a doorway, or carpet border, helps them learn what is acceptable. If you allow so much as a paw or whisker across, it quickly becomes a nose or a leg, followed by the whole dog in inches; before you know it, they are under the table, or more likely, jostling your elbow. It is not wise to feed your Weimaraner from your plate or from the table. The first time you give in to those soulful eyes will seal your fate. It only takes once for a Weimaraner to know where the bread is buttered, and the habit of begging is terribly difficult to break. Besides, most of the food we eat is really not too nutritious for our dogs, and upsets his regular eating habits.

TO SUPPLEMENT OR NOT TO SUPPLEMENT?

If you're feeding your dog a diet that's correct for his developmental stage and he's alert, healthy-looking and neither over- nor underweight, you don't need to add supplements. These include table scraps as well as vitamins and minerals. In fact, unless you are a nutrition expert, using food supplements can actually hurt a growing puppy. For example, mixing too much calcium into your dog's food can lead to musculoskeletal disorders. Educating yourself about the quantity of vitamins and minerals your dog needs to be healthy will help you determine what needs to be supplemented. If you have any concerns about the nutritional quality of the food you're feeding, discuss them with your veterinarian.

Supplementation

What a tricky subject! Most commercial kibbles will provide the average dog a balanced diet without additional supplementation. In recent years, however, the standards set by the American Association of Feed Control Officials have been called into question. Additionally, not every dog is the average dog. Some dogs may not metabolize a particular protein or vitamin well enough, and may require supplementation.

If you are interested in the affects of your dog's diet on long-term health, there are now many books and articles available with which to educate yourself (the books by Dr. Pitcairn and Wendy Volhard referenced above to start with). Supplementation should *never* be undertaken without consultation with your veterinarian and a high level of self-education. Some vitamins can actually be toxic when present in high levels, particularly the fat soluble ones, such as A, E, and K. Not only is the amount of a particular vitamin or mineral important, its proportion in relation to other vitamins and minerals can be critical. For example, the ratios of calcium, phosphorus, and magnesium are just as important as the amounts. If you are feeding a homemade diet, it is critical that you read as much as possible on the subjects of vitamins, minerals, and supplementation to ensure that you get the right combination as well as ratios.

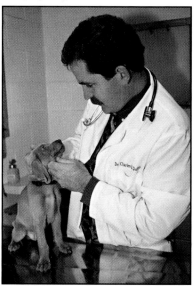

The subject of canine nutrition is a rapidly changing and advancing field. For the long-term health of your dog, become a label reader, and take whatever opportunities are available to become better educated on nutrition and its affect on your dog's health.

The wrong combination of supplements may do more harm than good.

chapter 6

Grooming
Your
Weimaraner

Every dog benefits from regular grooming, not just for appearance sake, but also for health reasons. Lucky for us, grooming a Weimaraner is relatively simple. They don't require any tricky clipping or extensive combing or brushing, but at least once a week, they do need to be groomed. During your weekly grooming session you will do more than just brush your dog; you will be training, examining and bonding with your dog. Best of all it isn't time consuming, maybe ten to fifteen minutes, once you get the hang of it. If you start out right, your dog will come to love it as much as you do.

Tools of the Trade

There isn't a great deal of equipment needed to groom your Weimaraner. A few items are necessary, while others are a convenience. Most of these products are available at your local pet supply store. For those who are really money conscious are several catalogs available that offer significant savings on pet supplies: Drs. Foster and Smith, R.C. Steele and New England Serum Company to name only a few.

BRUSHES

There is a bewildering array of brushes available at pet supply stores and catalogs. For a Weimaraner, all you really need in the way of brushes are a curry type brush and a bristle type brush. The rubber currycomb is ideal for removing the dead hair, especially during the seasonal shedding that does occur. The bristle type brush removes the accumulation of dust and surface dirt, and helps distribute the natural oils of the coat evenly. Today these can even be found with comfortable ergonomic handles or glove styles, so grooming is as comfortable for the owner as for the dog.

Weimaraners and their owners are lucky that brushing is a relatively simple task for this breed.

NAIL TRIMMERS

Do you hear "click, click, click" as your dog walks across a hard surface? Trimming your Weimaraner's nails is an absolute must. Even with plenty of exercise, a Weimaraner's nails can grow to uncomfortable lengths.

Weimaraners also like to paw things like your carpet, your leg, and your furniture. Keeping the nails trimmed and smooth will literally help reduce wear and tear. If you can hear them, you can trim them.

With practice, both you and your dog will breeze through nail trimming.

There are basically two different types of nail trimmers: guillotine and scissors type. For a large dog like the Weimaraner, I prefer a quality scissors type. The guillotine types just don't seem to hold up to the hard thick nails of this breed. If your nail clippers leave a ragged edge or crush the nail before cutting it, it is time to replace them. Another option is the grinder: a specialized hand tool with a sanding wheel. It is often difficult for an adult dog to become accustomed to grinders, but puppies started young don't seem to mind them.

If you are really afraid of over-trimming, a large file can also be used. Although it takes longer, almost any dog will learn to tolerate a file. Your veterinarian, or a local Weimaraner breeder probably won't mind showing you just how to trim your dog's nails.

QUICK AND PAINLESS NAIL CLIPPING

This is possible if you make a habit out of handling your dog's feet and giving your dog treats when you do. When it's time to clip nails, go through the same routine, but take your clippers and snip off just the end of the nail—clip too far down and you'll cut into the "quick," the nerve center, hurting your dog and causing the nail to bleed. Clip two nails a session while you're getting your dog used to the procedure, and you'll soon be doing all four feet quickly and easily.

Along with nail trimmers you'll want to get some Kwik-stop or a similar product. Kwik-stop is a doggie styptic powder. Somewhere along the line you will trim a nail too close and it will bleed. Don't panic. Several products are available from powdered styptics like Kwik-stop to the superglue-like (never use regular superglue) Nexaband developed for surgical applications. In an emergency, you could use cornstarch or a bar of soap as well. Remember the next time to be a little extra patient to restore your dog's comfort level and trust.

TOOTHBRUSH

You need a toothbrush for your dog? Absolutely. Dental care for your dog is as important for her as it is for you. Although dogs rarely get cavities, they are subject to periodontal disease. Severe periodontal disease can result not only in the loss of teeth, but severely damage your dog's overall health as well, including heart and kidney damage. Daily brushing (or even weekly) brushing will help preserve your dog's healthy smile. Special toothbrushes are available. Some are just like regular brushes but softer and angled; others fit over the end of your finger. A regular people toothbrush will also work. When you brush, use toothpaste made for dogs (really!) because people toothpaste is too sudsy, and most dogs don't like the taste, additionally, the safety of fluoride in dogs has never really been studied. If you and your dog prefer not to use a toothbrush, the same effect can be achieved with plain or specially treated gauze pads.

Dental hygiene is as important to your dog as it is to you.

SHAMPOO

Just as with toothpaste, a shampoo made just for dogs is your best choice. Shampoos made for humans are a different pH than those made for dogs and human shampoos may dry your dog's coat and skin. If you live in an area where fleas and ticks are a problem, a shampoo can be a part of your pest control program. When you bathe your dog, make sure the footing in the tub is secure to avoid frightening or possibly injuring your dog. Lots of treats can make bath time fun. Unless it is high summer, be sure to protect your dog from chills until she is completely dry. Keep an eye on your wet Weimaraner too. It is a toss-up as to which bed she will head for: your bed or the flowerbed.

Unless fleas are a problem, or you are competing, your dog will rarely need a bath. Excessive bathing will remove essential oils from your dog's skin and coat, resulting in a dry, brittle coat, and flaky skin. If your Weimaraner has excessively oily skin, or a strong "doggy" smell, discuss the potential of a dietary or medical problem with your veterinarian.

Teaching Your Dog to Love Grooming

Weimaraners don't need much grooming, but they do need some. But just as important while grooming, you will also be looking for signs of problems: ticks, fleas, cuts, lumps, smelly ears, bad breath, hot spots, what-

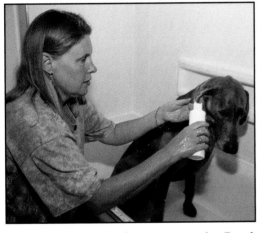

ever. If your dog enjoys the process, it is much easier. The key to helping your dog learn to enjoy this time together is to establish a reward history and to be patient. Don't expect your young puppy to stand up on the table and submit to an entire grooming session the first time. Break each

Use a shampoo specially formulated for dogs to keep your Weimaraner's coat looking its best.

part down separately. Brushing, for example: One stroke gets one (tiny) treat. If your puppy grabs the brush, stop moving it. If she continues, gently remove the brush from her mouth. But you should be quick enough to get a gentle swipe in before she has a chance to react. As soon as you stroke the brush, give her a treat. After a few strokes, quit for a while. When one stroke is no problem, work your way up to two strokes for each treat. Pretty soon your dog will be overjoyed to see the brush.

Soon you will be able to lift your puppy onto the table, do a short bit of brushing, or a single nail. Always stop before your dog gets restless. End each session on a positive note and some aspect of grooming that your dog enjoys, a good ear scratch and lots of praise and treats before you lift her off the table or release her from the grooming. Eventually you can work your way up to a full grooming session. In the end, you and your dog will look forward to the time you spend together.

Coat and Skin

Grooming your Weimaraner includes a thorough examination of her coat and skin. Some Weimaraners are prone to hot spots (a type of dermatitis) or lick granulomas. Hot spots occur in warm moist areas, such as the armpits, groin area, or under the collar. While they are not usually serious, hot spots can grow rapidly and should be treated promptly. Usually an antibacterial wash (or, for the homeopathic minded, apple cider vinegar) and keeping the area dry will remedy the problem.

Lick granulomas are caused by compulsive licking of a particular spot. Lick granulomas are most frequently found on the tops of the forelegs and feet. The dog licks the same spot until the hair is worn away. If left untreated, the skin soon becomes abraded as well. This behavior is often a result of boredom. Successful treatment requires preventing the dog from licking the affected area until it has a chance to heal completely. If the spot is identified before the skin has become abraded, sometimes a bitter apple spray, or cider vinegar, will prevent further damage. It is usually necessary to spray all four legs to discourage the dog from simply turning her attention to another spot. At the same time offer additional exercise and mental stimulation, and discourage licking behavior. Ulcerated skin may require veterinary attention and stronger measures to prevent further damage.

GROOMING TOOLS
pin brush
slicker brush
flea comb
towel
mat rake
grooming glove
scissors
nail clippers
tooth-cleaning equipment
shampoo
conditioner
clippers

While you are brushing your dog, check the base of the tail and the belly button area for fleas or telltale black specks of flea dirt. If you aren't sure if it's regular dirt or flea dirt, brush a little onto a paper towel and spray it with a little water from a misting sprayer. Flea dirt will turn a reddish color. Fleas not only cause you and your dog discomfort, they can also spread parasites, so flea control is a very important part of your pet's health. Fleas can cause irritation to your dog's skin and start a vicious cycle of scratching that may require veterinary intervention. Some dogs even develop an actual allergic response.

Also be on the lookout for foxtails and burrs. Because the Weimaraner's short coat does not offer a lot of protection from this type of hazard, you need to be vigilant. Foxtails and burrs can work their way in through the skin, between the toes, in the mouth or ears, causing your dog extreme discomfort. Discovered quickly, they are easy to remove from the Weimaraner's short coat; neglected, they may result in expensive veterinary treatment, even surgery.

Be sure to inspect your Weimaraner's coat thoroughly during your grooming session. Be on the lookout for fleas and ticks as well as skin problems like hot spots.

Nails

Trimming the nails is often a major issue for dogs. But it is usually a problem created by the owners, expecting too much too soon, or cutting nails too short and causing the dog pain early in the learning process. Nails that go untrimmed can grow to great lengths, making them vulnerable to injury. Long nails are more easily torn or damaged. Excessively long nails can even cause deformities of the toes and feet, in addition to making walking painful. Start young, and err on the side of caution when trimming nails. In fact, start by not trimming at all. Just get your puppy used to having her feet handled. Hold the paw in your hand, immediately give the puppy a treat, and let go. If puppy pulls away or bites at your hand, no treat. When there is no resistance, hold the paw a little longer. Step by step work your way up to handling each toe separately. When you get out the nail trimmers, let your puppy check them out, then just touch the trimmer to the toe and give your puppy a treat until she is comfortable with the procedure. The first time you trim, do only a single toe and take off just the tip. Be sure not to squeeze the paw too tightly. Hold it only firmly enough to keep it steady. If you squeeze too hard, your dog will pull away, and will soon learn to pull her paw away as soon as you take hold of it. Throughout the day you will eventually get all the nails, and puppy has learned that nail trimming means good things.

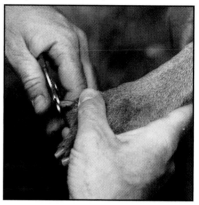

Start nail trimming young and make it lots of fun. This definitely pays big dividends in the long run. It may sound like a lot of trouble to begin with, but there is a world of difference between having your dog eagerly waiting to have her nails trimmed and having her run and hide at the sight of the trimmers, not to mention fighting you for each clip.

Trim your dog's nails before they get long enough to tear or break, causing great pain to your dog.

Teeth

Again, if you start brushing her teeth when your dog is a puppy, it is much easier to accustom her to the procedure. But even adult dogs can learn to at least tolerate having their teeth cleaned, if you take it slow and easy. Don't expect too much at first. If your dog is very resistant, start with getting her to let you look at her teeth. Gently cradle her chin in your hand. Be sure not to completely block your dog's vision by using your thumb and forefinger of the other hand on either side of the muzzle, lift the lip in the area of the small premolars behind the large canines for just a second. Immediately supply a simple scratch under the chin or behind the ears and a "Good girl," for a reward. Repeat over and over until your dog thinks nothing of it. This is something you can do while you are watching TV or sitting around talking. Gradually increase the time, and then start looking at the large molars in back of the pre-molars, and then forward to the incisors in the front. Remember to be gentle when lifting the lips, especially in the front under the nose. When your dog is accustomed to having her teeth looked at, you can begin with one or two gentle swipes with the gauze pad wrapped around your finger or a toothbrush. The flavored toothpaste makes an additional reward. If you are slow and patient, your dog will not only learn to tolerate it, she may even come to enjoy it!

While you are brushing, check for broken teeth, swollen gums, growths, and bad breath. Any of these conditions may warrant a visit to the vet. Your veterinarian will greatly appreciate a dog that is at least used to having her mouth handled, and it will benefit your dog's health as well. Almost all dogs will need to have their teeth cleaned at some point in their lives. Regular brushing at home can minimize the necessity of veterinary intervention and save you money.

Cleaning your Weimaraner's ears is another routine part of grooming your dog.

Ears

Some dogs, particularly those with dropped ears like the Weimaraner, may be prone to ear infections. Check your dog's ears frequently, especially if you notice an unusual amount of head shaking or ear scratching. A quick sniff may reveal a strong or foul odor, or the inside of the ear may appear red and swollen, but not always. Even if the ear looks fine, if your dog is frequently scratching or shaking her head, have your vet check it out. Even if it is not an infection, all that head shaking can result in a hematoma, a condition addressed in Chapter 7, "Keeping Your Weimaraner Healthy."

A gauze pad with a little ear cleaning solution, or cider vinegar, is great for cleaning the dirt and debris that sometimes accumulate in the outer area of the ear. It shouldn't be necessary for you to probe deeply in the ear canal to clean your dog's ears.

Eyes

Check your Weimaraner's eyes for excessive tearing or discharge. Although Weimaraners are generally not prone to eye problems, eye infections or injuries need prompt attention to prevent them from becoming serious. Excessive tearing may be a sign of entropion/ectropion (disorders of the eyelid) or trichiasis/distichiasis (disorder of the eyelashes). These conditions may be congenital or acquired and may possibly require veterinary treatment. Older dogs of most breeds can develop cataracts or glaucoma.

A Grooming Session

Because grooming a Weimaraner doesn't take very long, it may be most convenient to do it all at once; but if you like, you can break each part down and do them at separate times. A typical grooming session literally goes from nose to toes.

Examine the head area, including nose, mouth, eyes and ears. Brush the teeth. Clean the ears if necessary. Massage every inch of your dog's skin including legs, belly, and genital area looking for small injuries, sore spots, or lumps. Examine the feet, looking between toes, and checking pads and pasterns. Trim nails. Brush your dog thoroughly with the curry brush during shedding season. Finish off with the bristle brush, including legs and tail. If your dog's coat is excessively dry or sun-damaged, apply a coat conditioner. If you follow this routine, your dog will look great and you will know if anything unusual is going on with your dog's health.

Although all of these things should be done at least once a week, they don't all have to be done at once. Eyes, ears, and teeth can be examined during a commercial break while you watch TV. Brushing can be done while you do the laundry. Brush your dog's teeth after you brush your own. One of the great things about this breed is that their grooming is so simple.

chapter 7

Keeping Your Weimaraner Healthy

Choosing a Veterinarian

One of the first things you will do when you bring your puppy home is visit the vet for a health checkup. Your relationship with your veterinarian is critically important to the health of your pet. If you are not comfortable with the veterinarian, you may put off calling when you should, so don't hesitate to shop around. Ask friends and neighbors who they go to; but remember, the right vet for them may not be the right one for you. Ask why they like a particular veterinarian, and what they think of the staff as well. You will spend at least as much time talking to the staff as you do to the vet. Ask what their emergency and after-hours policies are. Most veterinarians will be glad to spend a few minutes talking to you (without your dog) to get to know them a little better. It's a good idea to check on prices too. While prices are not necessarily a sign of good or bad service, if you can't afford them, you need to either reconsider getting a dog, or find a vet whose services you can afford. And just because they are the

most expensive doesn't necessarily indicate the best service. It is your *relationship* that counts. At some point you may have to make life and death decisions based on how much you trust this person, so take your time until you feel the veterinarian is the right one for you.

Establishing a relationship with a particular veterinary practice helps you manage your dog's health as well. By visiting the same practice on a regular basis, they will have an ongoing picture of your dog's health. This will enable them to be on the alert for potential or developing problems, and to provide you with reminders for things like vaccinations, heartworm checks, regular dental care, and routine checkups. If you skip around from one veterinarian to another, you may miss out on this important benefit.

> ### YOUR PUPPY'S VACCINES
>
> Vaccines are given to prevent your dog from getting infectious diseases like canine distemper or rabies. Vaccines are the ultimate preventive medicine: They're given before your dog ever gets the disease to protect him from the disease. That's why it is necessary for your dog to be vaccinated routinely. Puppy vaccines start by 8 weeks of age for the five-in-one DHLPP vaccine and are given every three to four weeks until the puppy is 16 months old. Your veterinarian will put your puppy on a proper schedule and will remind you when to bring in your dog for shots.

The First Visit

If possible, avoid any vaccinations on the first visit because as far as your puppy is concerned, first impressions can be lasting ones. At this visit, the vet will do a general health checkup to look for signs of any illness or congenital problems that may not be obvious. He will listen to your puppy's heart and lungs and check all his joints, his eyes and ears. This is all petting as far as your puppy is concerned and makes your puppy feel a little more comfortable in this sometimes scary environment. Take a bag full of treats so that all the staff can give your puppy tasty tidbits and pet him. Make this trip fun! Try to schedule your appointment for a less busy time of the day so everyone will have time to admire and pet your puppy. A check for internal parasites is in order at this time, so treatment can get started right away. By the time your pup is ready to go in for his next vaccination, another check can be made to make sure they are gone.

Ounce of Prevention

You play the most important role in your dog's health care. By knowing what is normal for your dog, you can

Weimaraners need regular health checkups to keep them looking and feeling their best.

spot potential trouble before it becomes serious. If your dog seems lethargic, or out of sorts, you can start looking for possible causes; a closer examination might reveal a broken tooth or the beginnings of an abscess. Continued aberrant behavior, without apparent cause, may lead you to consult your veterinarian. But it is your being in tune with your dog that keeps him in tiptop shape. An ounce of prevention is truly worth a pound of cure. Not only can it save your dog from discomfort or long-term health problems, it can save you money as well. A veterinary office call and a single prescription are definitely more cost effective than waiting until more expensive and extensive treatment is necessary.

The single most cost-effective action you can take is feeding your dog the best possible diet to allow him to keep himself healthy. Be sure to read through Chapter 5, "Feeding Your Weimaraner."

Regular checkups are important for keeping your Weimaraner healthy too. Your veterinarian will give your dog a thorough examination to look for anything unusual you may have missed. He will also ask you questions that may indicate potential problems. Screening for parasites at least once a year can be performed in conjunction with your annual or semi-annual visit. Your vet will likely request a fresh stool sample to check for intestinal parasites, and draw a blood sample to look for heartworms. Although most veterinarians are satisfied if you come in once a year for vaccinations, there are great benefits to semi-annual visits. First, your dog is getting a thorough examination twice a year. A lot can change in a year. If your dog begins to succumb to a chronic illness shortly after your annual visit, it may have a full twelve months to progress before your next annual visit. A lot of damage can be done in that time. Second, recent research indicates that we may be over-taxing our dogs' immune systems by vaccinating them for four to ten different diseases at once. This can be slightly minimized by splitting the vaccinations into two groups.

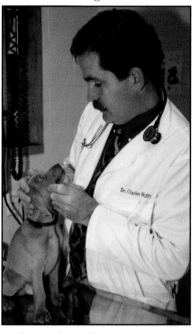

A good relationship with the veterinarian is the first step to keeping your puppy healthy.

Speaking of vaccinations . . . By the time you bring your puppy home, he may already be on a vaccination schedule. When you pick up your puppy, you should receive a record of the vaccinations and wormings that have already been given and a suggested schedule for remaining ones. Your puppy started out life getting important antibodies from his mother's milk. As he grows, this immunity will fade. Vaccinations challenge your puppy's immune system to produce antibodies to fight off potentially serious or deadly diseases. It is important that you continue these vaccinations until your puppy's system is able to maintain this immunity itself. Each puppy matures at different rates in this respect so a series of vaccinations spread over his first 6 months of life is necessary to maintain immunity. Later in this chapter the implications of vaccinations and the scheduling of vaccinations will be discussed. For now, suffice it to say that vaccinations are a necessary part of your puppy's life.

Parasites

The very idea of parasites in your puppy is pretty disconcerting. Yuck! Parasites drain your dog's vitality and reduce his ability to fight off illness. No one wants to spend money feeding parasites when what you really want to do is feed your dog. Untreated, some of these parasites can cause lasting damage to your dog's health, and sometimes even death. Although it is nearly impossible to prevent a properly socialized dog from ever being exposed to parasites; in this day and age, it is unthinkable that your dog should suffer from them for very long or contract them often.

Intestinal parasites can be easily picked up anywhere dogs frequent, and dogs simply can't resist investigating the best places to contract them. You might suspect parasites if your dog's coat begins to look dry and dull, your dog has frequent diarrhea or shows a marked loss of weight with an increase in appetite. Tapeworms, contracted most frequently from fleas, are easily spotted in your dog's stool or around the anal area; they look similar to grains of rice. Discourage your dog from visiting or sniffing areas frequently used for elimination by strange dogs, and encourage your dog to eliminate at home where you can pick it up immediately. Safe and effective treatments are available through your veterinarian if your dog does contract intestinal parasites.

"Parasites— yuck!" These pests are more than a nuisance— they are a major threat to your Weimaraner's health.

Heartworms may be contracted when an infected mosquito bites your dog. Larvae migrate through the dog's system, passing through several stages. As adults, they migrate and settle in to mature in the heart and large arteries and veins of your dog. As the heartworms grow, they may begin to physically block the circulation of blood, and cause strain on the heart. Adult worms can grow as long as twelve inches. Signs of heartworms include panting or shortness of breath, coughing, a general lack of fitness, and loss of weight. Although it is possible to treat your dog only during mosquito season, prevention is not that expensive. For most people it is much easier to remember to give the treatment every month, or every day, than to remember to start it up in the spring. Additionally, an unusual warm spell or early spring may result in an unexpected mosquito population. Treatment for heartworms is complex and dangerous; prevention is definitely the best choice. Daily and monthly treatments are available to prevent and treat heartworms. Some of these treatments also take care of hookworms, roundworms and whipworms as well.

External parasites such as fleas and ticks can also effect your dog's overall health as well as making your dog and you uncomfortable. A healthy dog is less attractive to fleas and ticks. If fleas and ticks are a problem where you live, discuss the new flea and tick control products now available. Some are administered as a pill, others are a liquid applied to the dog's skin between the shoulder blades. Several offer thirty days of protection even if your dog gets wet.

Sprays are also available. These can be applied before or after excursions to infested areas. But use these with caution! If a little works, more is not better. Use only the minimum necessary to control the problem; excessive exposure can

> **FLEAS AND TICKS**
>
> There are so many safe, effective products available now to combat fleas and ticks that—thankfully—these pests are less of a problem. Prevention is key, however. Ask your veterinarian about starting your puppy on a flea/tick repellent right away. With this, regular grooming and environmental controls, your dog and your home should stay pest-free. Without this attention, you risk infesting your dog and your home, and you're in for an ugly and costly battle to clear up the problem.

result in serious health problems for your dog. If you are using a topical monthly flea control, sprays are not only unnecessary, they may result in toxic reactions. Consult your veterinarian if the monthly treatment is ineffective. In some dogs the use of brewer's yeast may help control fleas.

If your dog does develop a flea problem, it is not enough to treat just your dog. The entire premises must be treated. Consult your veterinarian for effective treatments. When living in an area where fleas were a problem, I used whole house treatments twice a year as a preventive measure. Along with other aggressive preventive measures (frequent vacuuming, brushing with a flea comb, brewer's yeast, diatomaceous earth, and judicious spraying), we were able to eliminate fleas from our dogs and home, even during a summer when all those around us where scratching incessantly.

Genetics and Disease

In general, Weimaraners are a healthy breed, but there are a few problems that Weimaraner owners need to be aware of. Elbow and hip dysplaysia (HD) are not uncommon among most large breeds. And while the problem is not extremely widespread among Weimaraners, it does occur. Dysplaysia results in abnormal wear of the joint. Clinical symptoms include lameness and pain. An x-ray is required for accurate diagnosis. Prevention is a key factor. There seems to be

Every breed has its own set of health concerns, but Weimaraners are a generally healthy breed.

a strong genetic link in whether or not a dog will develop hip dysplaysia. A dog is more likely to develop this potentially crippling condition if his parents had it, and even more likely to develop it if siblings (littermates or half siblings) show signs. So look for a breeder that x-rays all breeding stock and gets OFA, ABVRA, or PennHip ratings. This is a good start in preventing your puppy from carrying the trait. Genetics is not the only factor though; environmental factors are at least as important as genetics. As an owner, you also contribute to prevention. Overweight puppies and dogs are more prone to develop HD. A balanced diet, with the correct ratio of calcium, phosphorous, and magnesium is also essential. Young dogs who are frequently on slick surfaces, or whose bones and joints are overly stressed by excessive exercise show a predisposition to HD. Avoid slick surfaces, highly demanding sports, jogging or jumping on hard surfaces or physical exertion beyond a young dog's abilities.

HD can range from mild to serious. In some dogs that are diagnosed with HD, you might never know. Others may be crippled before the age of 4 years. Several treatments are available to reduce your dog's discomfort if he is diagnosed with and develops clinical signs of hip dysplaysia, including medicines and exercise regimens. In severe circumstances, hip replacement surgery may be considered. In extreme cases, euthanasia may be considered. If your dog develops HD, contact your veterinarian or breeder.

Gastric Dilation and Volvulus

Bloat, technically called gastric dilation and volvulus, is a life threatening condition that occurs all too often in Weimaraners. One study listed the Weimaraner as third in a list of breeds most prone to bloat. Research has indicated that the number one cause of bloat is morphology, or the shape of the dog. The large size and deep chest of the Weimaraner predisposes them to this deadly occurrence.

When bloat begins, for whatever reason, the stomach begins to fill with gases released during the digestion of food—gastric dilation. The inflated stomach may then become twisted—volvulus or torsion. The swelling and twisting of the stomach results in the restriction of blood flow to several major organs including the stomach itself, the spleen and the heart. Eventually the dog goes into shock. Untreated, this condition will result in death. Complications after a bloat episode may have long-term consequences as well. The key to survival is early identification and treatment of the condition.

It appears that there are actually two types of bloat. One type is aerophagia, or the gulping of air while eating. Dogs that are extremely nervous or fearful are more prone to this problem. They often gulp their food down very quickly, aggravating the problem. Onset of symptoms is usually immediately following a meal—within minutes. Another type of bloat is more insidious and symptoms may not appear for more than an hour, even several hours after a meal.

Symptoms of bloat are unproductive vomiting, distension of the abdomen, panting, and restlessness. Tapping on the abdomen produces a distinctive drum like sound. The symptoms may become apparent within seconds or minutes of eating (aerophagia) or may not appear for an hour or even several hours after eating. As the condition progresses, the dog will become more and more uncomfortable. Your dog may become aggressive as a result of his pain, he may bite at his abdomen or he may cry and howl. As shock

Weimaraners are a breed prone to bloat, so be sure to know all the signs and symptoms to keep dinnertime from becoming a disaster.

approaches, the gums will become pale and slow to refill when pressed with a finger. Eventually the dog will lose consciousness.

If your dog displays symptoms of bloat, it is a medical emergency! Your dog is in serious danger! Do not attempt home treatment. Call your veterinarian or emergency service and notify them of your suspicion so they can be prepared for your arrival. Time is of the essence; research shows that the most critical factor in survival of bloat is timely diagnosis and initiation of treatment. Although it is sometimes possible to pass a stomach tube and relieve the pressure, surgery is the most likely possibility.

Also, be prepared to discuss preventive intervention. Once a dog has had an episode of bloat, it is highly likely that the dog will suffer a recurrence. The chances of survival decrease with each episode. Several highly successful procedures can be performed to reduce the likelihood of a recurrence. These generally involve attaching the stomach to the abdominal wall, using various techniques, to reduce the possibility of torsion of the stomach. Additional procedures reduce the possibility of gas accumulating in the stomach.

Although extensive research is ongoing, little is known about the actual cause and prevention of bloat and torsion. Researchers have pursued the possibility of a connection between particular ingredients such as soy or corn in foods, chemical preservatives, the type of food (canned compared to kibble), water consumption, and exercise. At this point there seems to be a familial connection, but it has yet to be conclusively proven. Bloat occurs more often in older dogs than young, and more often in males than in females. High-strung nervous dogs are more prone to bloat than mellow dogs. Over- and underweight dogs bloat more frequently than those of appropriate weight and fitness. Dogs on home-prepared diets are very slightly less prone to bloat than those on commercial diets.

Although not much has been proven, a few common sense rules apply until more is known. Ask the breeder about the incidence of bloat in the pedigree of any puppy you are considering. Avoid vigorous exercise after eating, as well as consumption of large amounts of water, to prevent the potential pendulum effect of a full stomach. A high quality, nutrient dense diet, fed twice daily reduces the amount of food in the stomach at any one time. In dogs that gulp their food very quickly, raising the bowl to chest height and reducing the size of meals (while feeding more frequently) may help.

Immune Deficiency Disorders

A growing health issue in Weimaraners, and other breeds as well, is immune dysfunction, or auto-immune deficiency. For as yet unknown reasons, a dog's immune system goes into overdrive. Symptoms are similar to those of a systemic infection: fever, elevated white blood cell counts, and swelling of the joints. Treatment at this time is supportive only, and may or may not be successful. Although genetics probably plays an important role, it is strongly believed that there is a link between vaccinations and the development of this devastating disorder. This is *not* a reason to not vaccinate your puppy. It is far more likely that your puppy may contract one of those diseases without proper immunization than he is to develop immune deficiency.

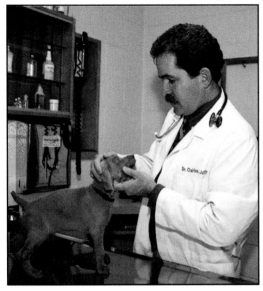

There is no perfect vaccination schedule, so work with your veterinarian to devise the best plan for your individual dog.

It is important to stress that there is no single perfect vaccination schedule. The decision of how and when to vaccinate can be influenced by many factors including, but not limited to, the breed, current health and location. It is a matter of professional judgment and choice. Your veterinarian's willingness to discuss this issue and its implication for your Weimaraner, however, may give you insight into how the future relationship may go with a particular veterinarian.

Spaying/Neutering

One of the most significant choices you will make for your Weimaraner is the decision to spay or neuter. Animal control facilities around the country are overwhelmed and purebred dogs are not exempt. Hundreds of thousands of animals are euthanized every year because homes cannot be found for them all. In some communities the problem is so serious that breeding has been banned completely, or huge licensing fees are required for intact dogs. Whether you plan to breed or not, if your dog (male or female) is intact they could potentially contribute to this problem.

Spaying and neutering may benefit the health of your dog. Spayed or neutered dogs have a decreased incidence of several diseases and illnesses. Certain types of cancer are reduced as much as 100%. It is physically impossible for a spayed female to suffer from potentially life threatening pyometra, an infection of the uterus.

Discuss the implications of spaying and neutering with your veterinarian. Unless you are planning on competing in field trials or conformation shows, the benefits of spaying and neutering generally far outweigh most other considerations.

First Aid

Weimaraners for the most part are curious, athletic, robust and rarely prone to illness. However, because of their curiosity and athletic nature, accidents are likely to occur at some point. Being prepared, and knowing how to deal with some basic possibilities will help you stay calm so that you can help your dog. The American Red Cross now offers classes in Pet First Aid and CPR, as well as a handy book.

ADVANTAGES OF SPAYING/NEUTERING

The greatest advantage of spaying (for females) or neutering (for males) is that you are guaranteed your dog will not produce puppies. There are too many puppies already available for too few homes. There are other advantages as well.

ADVANTAGES OF SPAYING

No messy heats.

No "suitors" howling at your windows or waiting in your yard.

No risk of pyometra (disease of the uterus) and decreased incidences of mammary cancer.

ADVANTAGES OF NEUTERING

Decreased incidences of fighting, but does not affect the dog's personality.

Decreased roaming in search of bitches in season.

Decreased incidences of many urogenital diseases.

Commercially prepared first aid kits are available, but you can make one fairly inexpensively also. For a basic kit, you need to include the following items for emergencies:

Rolled gauze

Gauze sponges in a variety of sizes

A large clean cloth

Muzzle

Compact thermal blanket

Eyewash

Chemical ice pack

Syrup of ipecac

Rectal thermometer

Diphenhydramine (talk to your vet about the correct dosage for your pet)

List of emergency numbers for your pet, including your veterinarian, the local emergency service, and the National Animal Poison Control (1-800-548-2423; there may be fees associated with calling this service)

These can be stored in a small box with your regular home first aid kit. Keep another in your car if your dog travels frequently with you. Check it each time you change the batteries in your smoke detector to make sure the items are in good condition.

Any time you are attempting first aid beyond the level of minor cuts on your dog, use a muzzle as long as the dog is not having respiratory difficulties. It seems inconceivable that your dog might attempt to bite you, but under the stress of fear and while in pain, any dog is unpredictable. Better safe than sorry. Inexpensive, compact, commercial muzzles are available, but a nylon stocking makes a great muzzle in an emergency, or even a leash. If you practice putting the muzzle on your dog before an emergency, you will know how to do it when it is necessary and you are pumped up with adrenaline. If you make it a pleasant experience with lots of praise then your dog will be comfortable with it too.

CUTS AND SCRAPES

The most common accidents to befall Weimaraners result from their insatiable curiosity and athletic nature. Cuts and scrapes are most frequent. Most can be treated at home with a triple antibiotic cream to prevent infection and reduce the possibility of the hair growing back white. If however, you cannot stop the bleeding with direct pressure within ten minutes, veterinary attention is likely required. Even small cuts should be observed for the possibility of infection. Watch for redness, swelling and tenderness, particularly of puncture wounds.

INTESTINAL OBSTRUCTION

Another common problem seen in Weimaraners is an intestinal obstruction. Weimaraners are known for picking up anything and everything, and if they can pick it up, they can swallow it. A few intestinal obstructions that I have seen include rocks, golf balls, keys, stockings, and coins. Although many times these items will pass through the dog's system,

Be prepared with a doggie first aid kit in case of emergencies. You have one for your family, and your puppy is an important new member now.

they may become lodged in the stomach or intestinal tract. Untreated they may cause death. My first Weimaraner died from a rock she swallowed, it was about the size of a quarter. Symptoms often include lethargy, vomiting, and decreased appetite; but the symptoms may be very mild. This is a situation where your observations may be critical in saving your dog's life. It is especially important to make sure dangerous objects are out of reach and appropriate chew toys are available for puppies.

Choking goes hand in hand with intestinal obstructions. Avoid the possibility by being a proactive owner. Take a Pet CPR/First Aid class from the American Red Cross so you will be prepared to deal with this emergency.

"Garbagitis"

Along with intestinal obstruction and choking, a discussion of "garbagitis" is in order. Weimaraners are notorious garbage can raiders; they just can't seem to understand why humans throw away such perfectly good stuff! Garbagitis is a very non-technical term for the consumption of spoiled, inappropriate or non-food items that may cause intestinal distress. It may be as simple as over-indulgence, or as serious as intestinal blockage. Don't take the chance. If you have a Weimaraner in the house, move your garbage and waste cans to secure locations. Inside a cupboard is your best bet. You may even need to put a child-proof latch on it. Weimaraners often mistake your efforts to protect them as a personal challenge.

Since your puppy will put just about anything that he physically can into his mouth, it is best to be vigilant to avoid intestinal obstruction and choking.

ELECTROCUTION

Electrocution from electrical cords is another mishap to which puppies in particular are prone. If you find your dog or puppy has been shocked and is still in contact with the cord, turn off the breaker before touching the dog! If the animal is unconscious, check for breathing and a heart beat. Perform CPR if necessary and you have the appropriate training. Veterinary attention is necessary even if your dog appears to be okay. Many complications can arise from electrical shock that are not immediately apparent.

HYPOTHERMIA

Because the Weimaraner loves to be active, but does not have a dense coat to protect him from the cold, awareness and prevention are necessary to prevent hypothermia. As in people, older dogs and young puppies are more susceptible. Unless it is extremely cold, most Weimaraners will deal with the cold by keeping active, but if they get wet or exhausted, they become vulnerable. In people, the symptoms are more easily observed, but dogs will also show uncontrollable shivering, dilated pupils, and decreased activity level and heart rates and possibly disorientation. As the body temperature continues to drop, shivering may stop and disorientation and lethargy may increase, or the dog may loose consciousness. If you suspect your dog is hypothermic, take him to a warmer (not hot) place. Remember that handy first aid kit? Take the dog's temperature rectally if you know how (if you don't know how, learn). If the temperature is below 100°F, your dog is in danger. Wrap the dog in warm blankets. If he is a puppy, hold him against your skin inside your shirt and wrap yourself in a blanket. Transport him to a veterinarian right away.

HEAT STROKE

Hyperthermia, or heat stroke, is not very frequently seen in Weimaraners. When it is, it is most often associated with dogs that have been left in cars. *Never* leave your dog unsupervised, even for a short time, in the car if the temperature is above 70°F. Even on a mild day, the temperature inside a car can quickly rise to over 120°F. Cracking the windows and parking in the shade may not protect your dog. Dogs kept on concrete runs, or left without shade and fresh, *cool* water are also vulnerable. Dogs that are unused to a warmer climate or exercising heavily on warm days may also become

WHEN TO CALL THE VETERINARIAN

In any emergency situation, you should call your veterinarian immediately. Try to stay calm when you call, and give the vet or the assistant as much information as possible before you leave for the clinic. That way, the staff will be able to take immediate, specific action when you arrive. Emergencies include:

- Bleeding or deep wounds
- Hyperthermia (overheating)
- Shock
- Dehydration
- Abdominal pain
- Burns
- Fits
- Unconsciousness
- Broken bones
- Paralysis

Call your veterinarian if you suspect any health problems.

Another potential danger associated with the Weimaraner's inquisitive nature is poisoning. Although you can't always be there, it's best to make sure that everything that goes in your puppy's mouth is safe.

victims of heatstroke. Dogs don't sweat the way people do. They depend on the rapid exchange of air while panting to keep them cool. When the air they are breathing is close to or higher than their body temperature they may be vulnerable to heat stroke.

Heat stroke is a medical emergency. Immediate action must be taken to prevent permanent damage or even death. Move the dog to a cooler location. If possible initiate cooling procedures while transporting the dog to the veterinarian. Take the dog's temperature if you know how. Spray the animal with cool water or cover with towels soaked in cool water. Direct a fan over the dog, or use anything handy to increase airflow and encourage evaporation. After five minutes, retake the dog's temperature. Once the dog's temperature is below 104°F stop the cooling process. If the dog has not collapsed from heatstroke, he may go into shock from the cooling process. Once the dog's temperature is below 104°F, it is still necessary that he be seen by a veterinarian.

Their curious nature and tendency to pick up almost anything they find exposes many Weimaraners to the possibility of poisoning. The most common symptoms of poisoning are excessive salivation, vomiting and/or diarrhea (with or without blood), seizures, trembling, unusual excitability or depression, or unexplained loss of consciousness. Poisoning may result from the direct consumption of a poisonous substance, or indirectly, from licking a substance off the feet or fur, or consuming another animal (such as a rat or gopher) that has been poisoned.

If you suspect poisoning, call your veterinarian immediately. The national or local poison control center would be your second bet. Do not induce vomiting unless directed to do so by your veterinarian or the poison control center. Transport the dog to your veterinarian or emergency facility as quickly as possible. Keep your pet as still and calm as possible. If possible, take the container for the poison along with you if you can do so safely. The container may provide important information for treatment.

Once again, prevention is important. Avoid keeping poisonous materials around your home whenever possible. When necessary, keep such substances stored in upper, lockable cabinets. Some poisonous substances commonly found in the home are fertilizer, antifreeze, rat poison, slug bait, and cleaning solutions. For dogs, chocolate is as dangerous as many poisons and should be treated as such: locked away high out of reach.

These issues address the most common emergencies Weimaraner owners may face. Please purchase and read a book on emergency first aid for pets. Your knowledge and quick actions may save your pet's life.

EAR HEMATOMAS

Ear hematomas frequently result from excessive shaking of the head. The tissue of the earflap is damaged (not the inner ear itself) and becomes engorged with blood and fluid. Although not life-threatening by any stretch of the imagination, if left untreated, the healing process usually leaves the ear malformed. Without treatment the condition will usually recur frequently. The hematoma can also rupture, which could be potentially dangerous as well as extremely messy. Although not usually painful, hematomas are decidedly uncomfortable for the dog. It is not uncommon for the edges of the ears to become slightly ragged and

91

thickened from slight injuries resulting from head shaking. This should not be confused with a hematoma.

IDENTIFY YOUR DOG

It is a terrible thing to think about, but your dog could somehow, someday, get lost or be stolen. How would you get him back? Your best bet would be to have some form of identification on your dog. You can choose from a collar and tags, a tattoo, a microchip or a combination of these three.

Every dog should wear a buckle collar with identification tags. They are the quickest and easiest way for a stranger to identify your dog. It's best to inscribe the tags with your name and phone number; you don't need to include your dog's name.

There are two ways to permanently identify your dog. The first is a tattoo, placed on the inside of your dog's thigh. The tattoo should be your social security number or your dog's AKC registration number.

The second is a microchip, a rice-sized pellet that is inserted under the dog's skin at the base of the neck, between the shoulder blades. When a scanner is passed over the dog, it will beep, notifying the person that the dog has a chip. The scanner will then show a code, identifying the dog. Microchips are becoming more and more popular and are certainly the wave of the future.

Going on Vacation

When I dog-sit for friends who are on vacation, I always ask for a letter authorizing me to request veterinary treatment for their dog. In the letter they not only give permission for me to seek treatment, but also indicate that they will accept responsibility for payment and to what extent. I also ask them to call their veterinarian ahead of time and tell him that I will be caring for their pet.

Old and Gray

As your dog matures and ages you will begin to see signs of old age. Lower activity levels and stiffness in the joints may be seen in dogs after the age of 7 or 8, but sometimes not until much later. As your dog ages be sure to monitor his weight. Obesity stresses older organs and joints even more than in younger dogs. Lower activity levels may necessitate a reduction in calories. Discuss changing your dog over to a diet formulated for senior dogs with your veterinarian at your semi-annual visit. Some experts are suggesting that older dogs may not need to be vaccinated as frequently, especially if they are not in tiptop health. If your dog is showing signs of stiffness in the joints, consider a supplement of chondroiton and glucosimine supplement. Making sure your older dog has a warm, dry, comfortable place to rest and sleep in can also help reduce stiffness. Mild to moderate exercise, depending on your dog's condition, is also important for maintaining your dog's muscle mass, condition, and zest for living. As your dog ages, previously minor considerations take on greater importance. Dental care is even more important. So is keeping nails trimmed. If you have started your young dog out with regular attention to his teeth and toes, you should simply continue as part of your routine now.

Just because your dog is maturing doesn't mean she's no longer a terrific pet.

Older dogs sometimes suffer from urinary incontinence, especially spayed females. Not only is this inconvenient and troublesome for you, many dogs are distressed by the problem as well! Make sure your dog has access to appropriate areas for urination frequently. If incontinence becomes a problem, talk to your veterinarian; many drug therapies are available for successful treatment of this problem.

Fatty and fibrous tumors are not unusual in aging Weimaraners. These growths are usually slow growing and move freely beneath the skin's surface. Although it is usually not necessary or practical to remove them, you will want to keep an eye on any growths. If they begin to interfere with freedom of movement, eating, or breathing they may need to be removed. Malignant tumors are not common in Weimaraners. They are frequently characterized by rapid growth, ulcerated areas, and do not move freely under the skin. Any growth should be brought to the attention of your veterinarian at your semi-annual visit; your veterinarian should examine suspicious growths as soon as possible.

Many older Weimaraners pass away quietly in their sleep; however, you may have to make a difficult decision about your pet's welfare. The decision to continue treatment or to end your dog's suffering is a highly personal one. This is when your relationship with your veterinarian is priceless. Discuss the practicality and expense of treatment, as well as the quality of life, and how much time the treatment will "buy" your dog. It is not reasonable to bankrupt yourself to add 6 months of misery to your dog's life. If treatment requires medication you are unable to administer, then euthanasia may be a consideration.

Immediately after the loss of a pet is not the time to consider a new puppy for most people. Getting a puppy needs to be a well-considered, well-planned process. I can think of few things as empty as a house without a dog in it—in the midst of grieving it may be very difficult to say no to a puppy that may not quite be the right one for you and your family.

It is often helpful to have a friend to talk to about your dog and your memories and feelings. I would be willing to bet that nearly anyone else who has ever owned and lost a Weimaraner will lend you a willing ear. It often helps if you can do something to memorialize your friend. You may want to consider a donation in your pet's name to your local rescue organization or an animal health research program such as the Morris Foundation.

Your Happy, Healthy Pet

Your Dog's Name _____

Name on Your Dog's Pedigree (if your dog has one) _____

_____

Where Your Dog Came From _____

_____

Your Dog's Birthday _____

Your Dog's Veterinarian

    Name _____

    Address _____

    Phone Number_____

    Emergency Number_____

Your Dog's Health

    Vaccines

    type _____ date given _____

    type _____ date given _____

    type _____ date given _____

    type _____ date given _____

    Heartworm

    date tested _____ type used_____ start date _____

Your Dog's License Number_____

Groomer's Name and Number _____

Dogsitter/Walker's Name and Number_____

Awards Your Dog Has Won

    Award _____ date earned _____

    Award _____ date earned _____

part three

Enjoying

your

Dog

chapter **8**

Basic
Training

by Ian Dunbar, Ph.D., MRCVS

Training is the jewel in the crown—the most important aspect of doggy husbandry. There is no more important variable influencing dog behavior and temperament than the dog's education: A well-trained, well-behaved and good-natured puppydog is always a joy to live with, but an untrained and uncivilized dog can be a perpetual nightmare. Moreover, deny the dog an education and she will not have the opportunity to fulfill her own canine potential; neither will she have the ability to communicate effectively with her human companions.

Luckily, modern psychological training methods are easy, efficient, effective and, above all, considerably dog-friendly and user-friendly.

Doggy education is as simple as it is enjoyable. But before you can have a good time play-training with your new dog, you have to learn what to do and how to do it. There is no bigger variable influencing the success of dog training than the *owner's* experience and expertise. *Before you embark on the dog's education, you must first educate yourself.*

Basic Training for Owners

Ideally, basic owner training should begin well *before* you select your dog. Find out all you can about your chosen breed first, then master rudimentary training and handling skills. If you already have your puppy-dog, owner training is a dire emergency—the clock is ticking! Especially for puppies, the first few weeks at home are the most important and influential days in the dog's life. Indeed, the cause of most adolescent and adult problems may be traced back to the initial days the pup explores her new home. This is the time to establish the *status quo*—to teach the puppydog how you would like her to behave and so prevent otherwise quite predictable problems.

In addition to consulting breeders and breed books such as this one (which understandably have a positive breed bias), seek out as many pet owners with your breed as you can find. Good points are obvious. What you want to find out are the breed-specific *problems,* so you can nip them in the bud. In particular, you should talk to owners with *adolescent* dogs and make a list of all anticipated problems. Most important, *test drive* at least half a dozen adolescent and adult dogs of your breed yourself. An 8-week-old puppy is deceptively easy to handle, but she will acquire adult size, speed and strength in just four months, so you should learn now what to prepare for.

Puppy and pet dog training classes offer a convenient venue to locate pet owners and observe dogs in action. For a list of suitable trainers in your area, contact the Association of Pet Dog Trainers (see chapter 13). You may also begin your basic owner training by observing other owners in class. Watch as many classes and test drive as many dogs as possible. Select an upbeat, dog-friendly, people-friendly, fun-and-games, puppydog pet training class to learn the ropes. Also, watch training videos and read training books. You must find out what to do and how to do it *before* you have to do it.

Principles of Training

Most people think training comprises teaching the dog to do things such as sit, speak and roll over, but even a 4-week-old pup knows how to do these things already. Instead, the first step in training involves teaching the dog human words for each dog behavior and activity and for each aspect of the dog's environment. That way you, the owner, can more easily participate in the dog's domestic education by directing her to perform specific actions appropriately, that is, at the right time, in the right place and so on. Training opens communication channels, enabling an educated dog to at least understand her owner's requests.

In addition to teaching a dog *what* we want her to do, it is also necessary to teach her *why* she should do what we ask. Indeed, 95 percent of training revolves around motivating the dog *to want to do* what we want. Dogs often understand what their owners want; they just don't see the point of doing it—especially when the owner's repetitively boring and seemingly senseless instructions are totally at odds with much more pressing and exciting doggy distractions. It is not so much the dog that is being stubborn or dominant; rather, it is the owner who has failed to acknowledge the dog's needs and feelings and to approach training from the dog's point of view.

The Meaning of Instructions

The secret to successful training is learning how to use training lures to predict or prompt specific behaviors—to coax the dog to do what you want *when* you want. Any highly valued object (such as a treat or toy) may be used as a lure, which the dog will follow with her eyes and nose. Moving the lure in specific ways entices the dog to move her nose, head and entire body in specific ways. In fact, by learning the art of manipulating various lures, it is possible to teach the dog to assume virtually any body position and perform any action. Once you have control over the expression of the dog's behaviors and can elicit any body position or behavior at will, you can easily teach the dog to perform on request.

Teach your dog words for each activity she needs to know, like down.

Tell your dog what you want her to do, use a lure to entice her to respond correctly, then profusely praise and maybe reward her once she performs the desired action. For example, verbally request "Tina, sit!" while you move a squeaky toy upwards and backwards over the dog's muzzle (lure-movement and hand signal), smile knowingly as she looks up (to follow the lure) and sits down (as a result of canine anatomical engineering), then praise her to distraction ("Gooood Tina!"). Squeak the toy, offer a training treat and give your dog and yourself a pat on the back.

Being able to elicit desired responses over and over enables the owner to reward the dog over and over. Consequently, the dog begins to think training is fun. For example, the more the dog is rewarded for sitting, the more she enjoys sitting. Eventually the dog comes to realize that, whereas most sitting is appreciated, sitting immediately upon request usually prompts especially enthusiastic praise and a slew of high-level rewards. The dog begins to sit on cue much of the time, showing that she is starting to grasp the meaning of the owner's verbal request and hand signal.

WHY COMPLY?

Most dogs enjoy initial lure-reward training and are only too happy to comply with their owners' wishes. Unfortunately, repetitive drilling without appreciative feedback tends to diminish the dog's enthusiasm until she eventually fails to see the point of complying anymore. Moreover, as the dog approaches adolescence she becomes more easily distracted as she develops other interests. Lengthy sessions with repetitive exercises tend to bore and demotivate both parties. If it's not fun, the owner doesn't do it and neither does the dog.

Integrate training into your dog's life: The greater number of training sessions each day and the *shorter* they are, the more willingly compliant your dog will

become. Make sure to have a short (just a few seconds) training interlude before every enjoyable canine activity. For example, ask your dog to sit to greet people, to sit before you throw her Frisbee and to sit for her supper. Really, sitting is no different from a canine "Please."

To train your dog, you need gentle hands, a loving heart and a good attitude.

Also, include numerous short training interludes during every enjoyable canine pastime, for example, when playing with the dog or when she is running in the park. In this fashion, doggy distractions may be effectively converted into rewards for training. Just as all games have rules, fun becomes training . . . and training becomes fun.

Eventually, rewards actually become unnecessary to continue motivating your dog. If trained with consideration and kindness, performing the desired behaviors will become self-rewarding and, in a sense, your dog will motivate herself. Just as it is not necessary to reward a human companion during an enjoyable walk in the park, or following a game of tennis, it is hardly necessary to reward our best friend—the dog— for walking by our side or while playing fetch. Human company during enjoyable activities is reward enough for most dogs.

Even though your dog has become self-motivating, it's still good to praise and pet her a lot and offer rewards once in a while, especially for a good job well done. And if for no other reason, praising and rewarding others is good for the human heart.

PUNISHMENT

Without a doubt, lure-reward training is by far the best way to teach: Entice your dog to do what you want and then reward her for doing so. Unfortunately, a human shortcoming is to take the good for granted and to moan and groan at the bad. Specifically, the dog's many good behaviors are ignored while the owner focuses on punishing the dog for making mistakes. In extreme cases, instruction is *limited* to punishing mistakes made by a trainee dog, child, employee or husband, even though it has been proven punishment training is notoriously inefficient and ineffective and is decidedly unfriendly and combative. It teaches the dog that training is a drag, almost as quickly as it teaches the dog to dislike her trainer. Why treat our best friends like our worst enemies?

Punishment training is also much more laborious and time consuming. Whereas it takes only a finite amount of time to teach a dog what to chew, for example, it takes much, much longer to punish the dog for each and every mistake. Remember, *there is only one right way!* So why not teach that right way from the outset?!

To make matters worse, punishment training causes severe lapses in the dog's reliability. Since it is obviously impossible to punish the dog each and every time she misbehaves, the dog quickly learns to distinguish between those times when she must comply (so as to avoid impending punishment) and those times when she need not comply, because punishment is impossible. Such times include when the dog is off leash and 6 feet away, when the owner is otherwise engaged (talking to a friend, watching television, taking a shower, tending to the baby or chatting on the telephone) or when the dog is left at home alone.

Instances of misbehavior will be numerous when the owner is away, because even when the dog complied in the owner's looming presence, she did so unwillingly. The dog was forced to act against her will, rather than molding her will to want to please. Hence, when the owner is absent, not only does the dog know she need not comply, she simply does not want to. Again, the trainee is not a stubborn vindictive beast, but rather the trainer has failed to teach. Punishment training invariably creates unpredictable Jekyll and Hyde behavior.

Trainer's Tools

Many training books extol the virtues of a vast array of training paraphernalia and electronic and metallic gizmos, most of which are designed for canine restraint, correction and punishment, rather than for actual facilitation of doggy education. In reality, most effective training tools are not found in stores; they come from within ourselves. In addition to a willing dog, all you really need is a functional human brain, gentle hands, a loving heart and a good attitude.

In terms of equipment, all dogs do require a quality buckle collar to sport dog tags and to attach the leash (for safety and to comply with local leash laws). Hollow chew toys (like Kongs or sterilized longbones) and a dog bed or collapsible crate are musts for housetraining. Three additional tools are required:

1. specific lures (training treats and toys) to predict and prompt specific desired behaviors;

2. rewards (praise, affection, training treats and toys) to reinforce for the dog what a lot of fun it all is; and

3. knowledge—how to convert the dog's favorite activities and games (potential distractions to training) into "life-rewards," which may be employed to facilitate training.

The most powerful of these is *knowledge*. Education is the key! Watch training classes, participate in training classes, watch videos, read books, enjoy play-training with your dog and then your dog will say "Please," and your dog will say "Thank you!"

Housetraining

If dogs were left to their own devices, certainly they would chew, dig and bark for entertainment and then no doubt highlight a few areas of their living space with sprinkles of urine, in much the same way we decorate by hanging pictures. Consequently, when we ask a dog to live with us, we must teach her *where* she may dig, *where* she may perform her toilet duties, *what* she may chew and *when* she may bark. After all, when left at home alone for many hours, we cannot expect the dog to amuse herself by completing crosswords or watching the soaps on TV!

Also, it would be decidedly unfair to keep the house rules a secret from the dog, and then get angry and punish the poor critter for inevitably transgressing rules she did not even know existed. Remember: Without adequate education and guidance, the dog will be forced to establish her own rules—doggy rules—and most probably will be at odds with the owner's view of domestic living.

Since most problems develop during the first few days the dog is at home, prospective dog owners must be certain they are quite clear about the principles of housetraining *before* they get a dog. Early misbehaviors quickly become established as the *status quo*—

becoming firmly entrenched as hard-to-break bad habits, which set the precedent for years to come. Make sure to teach your dog good habits right from the start. Good habits are just as hard to break as bad ones!

Ideally, when a new dog comes home, try to arrange for someone to be present as much as possible during the first few days (for adult dogs) or weeks for puppies. With only a little forethought, it is surprisingly easy to find a puppy sitter, such as a retired person, who would be willing to eat from your refrigerator and watch your television while keeping an eye on the newcomer to encourage the dog to play with chew toys and to ensure she goes outside on a regular basis.

POTTY TRAINING

To teach the dog where to relieve herself:

1. never let her make a single mistake;

2. let her know where you want her to go; and

3. handsomely reward her for doing so: "GOOOOOOOD DOG!!!" liver treat, liver treat, liver treat!

Preventing Mistakes

A single mistake is a training disaster, since it heralds many more in future weeks. And each time the dog soils the house, this further reinforces the dog's unfortunate preference for an indoor, carpeted toilet. *Do not let an unhousetrained dog have full run of the house.*

When you are away from home, or cannot pay full attention, confine the dog to an area where elimination is appropriate, such as an outdoor run or, better still, a small, comfortable indoor kennel with access to an outdoor run. When confined in this manner, most dogs will naturally housetrain themselves.

If that's not possible, confine the dog to an area, such as a utility room, kitchen, basement or garage, where elimination may not be desired in the long run but as an interim measure it is certainly preferable to doing it all around the house. Use newspaper to cover the floor of the dog's day room. The newspaper may be used to soak up the urine and to wrap up and dispose of the feces. Once your dog develops a preferred spot for eliminating, it is only necessary to cover that part of the floor with newspaper. The smaller papered area may then be moved (only a little each day) towards the door to the outside. Thus the dog will develop the tendency to go to the door when she needs to relieve herself.

Never confine an unhousetrained dog to a crate for long periods. Doing so would force the dog to soil the crate and ruin its usefulness as an aid for housetraining (see the following discussion).

Teaching Where

In order to teach your dog where you would like her to do her business, you have to be there to direct the proceedings—an obvious, yet often neglected, fact of life. In order to be there to teach the dog *where* to go, you need to know *when* she needs to go. Indeed, the success of housetraining depends on the owner's ability to predict these times. Certainly, a regular feeding schedule will facilitate prediction somewhat, but there is nothing like "loading the deck" and influencing the timing of the outcome yourself!

The first few weeks at home are the most important and influential in your dog's life.

Whenever you are at home, make sure the dog is under constant supervision and/or confined to a small

to lie down in her bed or basket. Alternatively, confine the dog to a crate (doggy den) or tie-down (a short,
18-inch lead that can be clipped to an eye hook in
the baseboard near her bed). Short-term close confinement strongly inhibits urination and defecation,
since the dog does not want to soil her sleeping area.
Thus, when you release the puppydog each hour, she
will definitely need to urinate immediately and defecate every third or fourth hour. Keep the dog confined to her doggy den and take her to her intended
toilet area each hour, every hour and on the hour.

When taking your dog outside, instruct her to sit quietly before opening the door—she will soon learn to sit
by the door when she needs to go out!

Teaching Why

Being able to predict when the dog needs to go enables the owner to be on the spot to praise and reward
the dog. Each hour, hurry the dog to the intended
toilet area in the yard, issue the appropriate instruction ("Go pee!" or "Go poop!"), then give the dog
three to four minutes to produce. Praise and offer a
couple of training treats when successful. The treats
are important because many people fail to praise their
dogs with feeling . . . and housetraining is hardly the
time for understatement. So either loosen up and enthusiastically praise that dog: "Wuzzzer-wuzzer-wuzzer,
hoooser good wuffer den? Hoooo went pee for
Daddy?" Or say "Good dog!" as best you can and offer
the treats for effect.

Following elimination is an ideal time for a spot of
play-training in the yard or house. Also, an empty dog
may be allowed greater freedom around the house for
the next half hour or so, just as long as you keep an eye
out to make sure she does not get into other kinds of
mischief. If you are preoccupied and cannot pay full
attention, confine the dog to her doggy den once more
to enjoy a peaceful snooze or to play with her many
chew toys.

If your dog does not eliminate within the allotted time outside—no biggie! Back to her doggy den, and then try again after another hour.

As I own large dogs, I always feel more relaxed walking an empty dog, knowing that I will not need to finish our stroll weighted down with bags of feces!

Beware of falling into the trap of walking the dog to get her to eliminate. The good ol' dog walk is such an enormous highlight in the dog's life that it represents the single biggest potential reward in domestic dogdom. However, when in a hurry, or during inclement weather, many owners abruptly terminate the walk the moment the dog has done her business. This, in effect, severely punishes the dog for doing the right thing, in the right place at the right time. Consequently, many dogs become strongly inhibited from eliminating outdoors because they know it will signal an abrupt end to an otherwise thoroughly enjoyable walk.

Instead, instruct the dog to relieve herself in the yard prior to going for a walk. If you follow the above instructions, most dogs soon learn to eliminate on cue. As soon as the dog eliminates, praise (and offer a treat or two)—"Good dog! Let's go walkies!" Use the walk as a reward for eliminating in the yard. If the dog does not go, put her back in her doggy den and think about a walk later on. You will find with a "No feces—no walk" policy, your dog will become one of the fastest defecators in the business.

If you do not have a backyard, instruct the dog to eliminate right outside your front door prior to the walk. Not only will this facilitate clean up and disposal of the feces in your own trash can but, also, the walk may again be used as a colossal reward.

CHEWING AND BARKING

Short-term close confinement also teaches the dog that occasional quiet moments are a reality of domestic living. Your puppydog is extremely impressionable during her first few weeks at home. Regular confinement at this time soon exerts a calming influence over the dog's personality. Remember, once the dog is housetrained and calmer, there will be a whole lifetime ahead for the dog to enjoy full run of the house and garden. On the other hand, by letting the newcomer have unrestricted access to the entire household and allowing her to run willy-nilly, she will most certainly develop a bunch of behavior problems in short order, no doubt necessitating confinement later in life. It would not be fair to remedially restrain and confine a dog you have trained, through neglect, to run free.

When confining the dog, make sure she always has an impressive array of suitable chew toys. Kongs and sterilized longbones (both readily available from pet stores) make the best chew toys, since they are hollow and may be stuffed with treats to heighten the dog's interest. For example, by stuffing the little hole at the top of a Kong with a small piece of freeze-dried liver, the dog will not want to leave it alone.

Remember, treats do not have to be junk food and they certainly should not represent extra calories. Rather, treats should be part of each dog's regular daily diet: Some food

Make sure your puppy has suitable chew toys.

may be served in the dog's bowl for breakfast and dinner, some food may be used as training treats, and some food may be used for stuffing chew toys. I regularly stuff my dogs' many Kongs with different shaped biscuits and kibble. The kibble seems to fall out fairly easily, as do the oval-shaped biscuits, thus rewarding the dog instantaneously for checking out the chew toys. The bone-shaped biscuits fall out after a while, rewarding the dog for worrying at the chew toy. But the triangular biscuits never come out. They remain inside the Kong as lures, maintaining the dog's fascination with her chew toy. To further focus the dog's interest, I always make sure to flavor the triangular biscuits by rubbing them with a little cheese or freeze-dried liver.

To teach come, call your dog, open your arms as a welcoming signal, wave a toy or a treat and praise for every step in your direction.

If stuffed chew toys are reserved especially for times the dog is confined, the puppydog will soon learn to enjoy quiet moments in her doggy den and she will quickly develop a chew-toy habit— a good habit! This is a simple *autoshaping* process; all the owner has to do is set up the situation and the dog all but trains herself— easy and effective. Even when the dog is given run of the house, her first inclination will be to indulge her rewarding chew-toy habit rather than destroy less-attractive household articles, such as curtains, carpets, chairs and compact disks. Similarly, a chew-toy chewer will be less inclined to scratch and chew herself excessively. Also, if the dog busies herself as a recreational chewer, she will be less inclined to develop into a recreational barker or digger when left at home alone.

Stuff a number of chew toys whenever the dog is left confined and remove the extra-special-tasting treats when you return. Your dog will now amuse herself with her chew toys before falling asleep and then resume playing with her chew toys when she expects you to return. Since most owner-absent misbehavior happens right after you leave and right before your expected return, your puppydog will now be conveniently preoccupied with her chew toys at these times.

Come and Sit

Most puppies will happily approach virtually anyone, whether called or not; that is, until they collide with adolescence and develop other more important doggy interests, such as sniffing a multiplicity of exquisite odors on the grass. Your mission, Mr./Ms. Owner, is to teach and reward the pup for coming reliably, willingly and happily when called—and you have just three months to get it done. Unless adequately reinforced, your puppy's tendency to approach people will self-destruct by adolescence.

Call your dog ("Tina, come!"), open your arms (and maybe squat down) as a welcoming signal, waggle a treat or toy as a lure and reward the puppydog when she comes running. Do not wait to praise the dog until she reaches you—she may come 95 percent of the way and then run off after some distraction. Instead, praise the dog's *first* step towards you and continue praising enthusiastically for *every* step she takes in your direction.

When the rapidly approaching puppy dog is three lengths away from impact, instruct her to sit ("Tina, sit!") and hold the lure in front of you in an outstretched hand to prevent her from hitting you midchest and knocking you flat on your back! As Tina decelerates to nose the lure, move the treat upwards and backwards just over her muzzle with an upwards motion of your extended arm (palm-upwards). As the dog looks up to follow the lure, she will sit down (if she jumps up, you are holding the lure too high). Praise the dog for sitting. Move backwards and call her again. Repeat this many times over, always praising when Tina comes and sits; on occasion, reward her.

For the first couple of trials, use a training treat both as a lure to entice the dog to come and sit and as a reward for doing so. Thereafter, try to use different items as lures and rewards. For example, lure the dog with a Kong or Frisbee but reward her with a food treat. Or lure the dog with a food treat but pat her and throw a tennis ball as a reward. After just a few repetitions, dispense with the lures and rewards; the dog will begin to respond willingly to your verbal requests and hand signals just for the prospect of praise from your heart and affection from your hands.

Instruct every family member, friend and visitor how to get the dog to come and sit. Invite people over for a series of pooch parties; do not keep the pup a secret— let other people enjoy this puppy, and let the pup enjoy other people. Puppydog parties are not only fun, they easily attract a lot of people to help *you* train *your* dog. Unless you teach your dog how to meet people, that is, to sit for greetings, no doubt the dog will resort to jumping up. Then you and the visitors will get annoyed, and the dog will be punished. This is not fair. *Send out those invitations for puppy parties and teach your dog to be mannerly and socially acceptable.*

Even though your dog quickly masters obedient recalls in the house, her reliability may falter when playing in the backyard or local park. Ironically, it is *the owner* who has unintentionally trained the dog *not* to respond in these instances. By allowing the dog to play and run around and otherwise have a good time, but then to call the dog to put her on leash to take her home, the dog quickly learns playing is fun but training is a drag. Thus, playing in the park becomes a severe distraction, which works against training. Bad news!

Instead, whether playing with the dog off leash or on leash, request her to come at frequent intervals—say, every minute or so. On most occasions, praise and pet the dog for a few seconds while she is sitting, then tell her to go play again. For especially fast recalls, offer a couple of training treats and take the time to praise and pet the dog enthusiastically before releasing her. The dog will learn that coming when called is not necessarily the end of the play session, and neither is it the end of the world; rather, it signals an enjoyable, quality time-out with the owner before resuming play once more. In fact, playing in the park now becomes a very effective life-reward, which works to facilitate training by reinforcing each obedient and timely recall. Good news!

Sit, Down, Stand and Rollover

Teaching the dog a variety of body positions is easy for owner and dog, impressive for spectators and extremely useful for all. Using lure-reward techniques, it is possible to train several positions at once to verbal commands or hand signals (which impress the socks off onlookers).

Sit and **down**—the two control commands—prevent or resolve nearly a hundred behavior problems. For example, if the dog happily and obediently sits or lies down when requested, she cannot jump on visitors, dash out the front door, run around and chase her tail, pester other dogs, harass cats or annoy family, friends or strangers. Additionally, "Sit" or "Down" are the best emergency commands for off-leash control.

It is easier to teach and maintain a reliable sit than maintain a reliable recall. *Sit* is the purest and simplest of commands—either the dog is sitting or she is not. If there is any change of circumstances or potential danger in the park, for example, simply instruct the dog to sit. If she sits, you have a number of options: Allow the dog to resume playing when she is safe, walk up and put the dog on leash or call the dog. The dog will be much more likely to come when called if she has already acknowledged her compliance by sitting. If the dog does not sit in the park—train her to!

Stand and **rollover-stay** are the two positions for examining the dog. Your veterinarian will love you to distraction if you take a little time to teach the dog to stand still and roll over and play possum. Also, your vet bills will be smaller because it will take the veterinarian less time to examine your dog. The rollover-stay is an especially useful command and is really just a variation of the down-stay: Whereas the dog lies prone in the traditional down, she lies supine in the rollover-stay.

As with teaching come and sit, the training techniques to teach the dog to assume all other body positions on cue are user-friendly and dog-friendly. Simply give the appropriate request, lure the dog into the desired body position using a training treat or toy and then *praise* (and maybe reward) the dog as soon as she complies. Try not to touch the dog to get her to respond. If you teach the dog by guiding her into position, the dog will quickly learn that rump-pressure means sit, for example, but as yet you still have no control over your dog if she is just 6 feet away. It will still be necessary to teach the dog to sit on request. So do not make training a time-consuming two-step process; instead, teach the dog to sit to a verbal request or hand signal from the outset. Once the dog sits willingly when requested, by all means use your hands to pet the dog when she does so.

To teach **down** when the dog is already sitting, say "Tina, down!," hold the lure in one hand (palm down) and lower that hand to the floor between the dog's forepaws. As the dog lowers her head to follow the lure, slowly move the lure away from the dog just a fraction (in front of her paws). The dog will lie down as she stretches her nose forward to follow the lure. Praise the dog when she does so. If the dog stands up, you pulled the lure away too far and too quickly.

When teaching the dog to lie down from the standing position, say "Down" and lower the lure to the floor as before. Once the dog has lowered her forequarters and assumed a play bow, gently and slowly move the lure *towards* the dog between her forelegs. Praise the dog as soon as her rear end plops down.

After just a couple of trials it will be possible to alternate sits and downs and have the dog energetically perform doggy push-ups. Praise the dog a lot, and after half a dozen or so push-ups reward the dog with a training treat or toy. You will notice the more energetically you move your arm—upwards (palm up) to get the dog to sit, and downwards (palm down) to get the dog to lie down—the more energetically the dog responds to your requests. Now try training the dog in silence and you will notice she has also learned to respond to hand signals. Yeah! Not too shabby for the first session.

To teach **stand** from the sitting position, say "Tina, stand," slowly move the lure half a dog-length away from the dog's nose, keeping it at nose level, and praise the dog as she stands to follow the lure. As soon

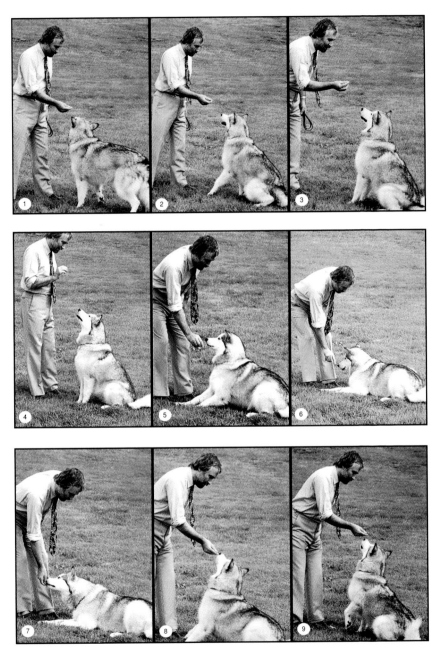

Using a food lure to teach sit, down and stand. 1) "Phoenix, sit." 2) Hand palm upwards, move lure up and back over dog's muzzle. 3) "Good sit, Phoenix!" 4) "Phoenix, down." 5) Hand palm downwards, move lure down to lie between dog's forepaws. 6) "Phoenix, off. Good down, Phoenix!" 7) "Phoenix, sit!" 8) Palm upwards, move lure up and back, keeping it close to dog's muzzle. 9) "Good sit, Phoenix!"

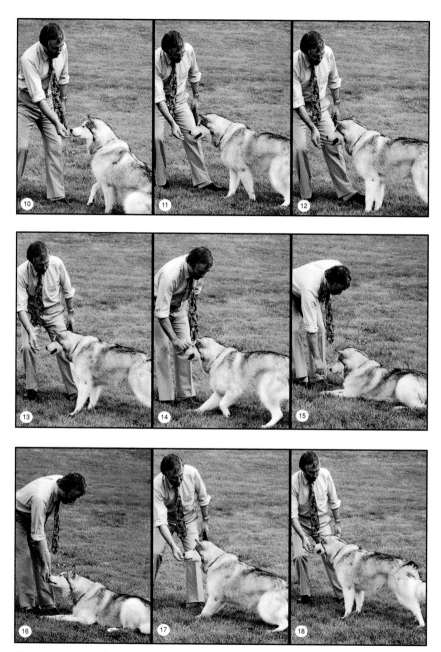

10) "Phoenix, stand!" 11) Move lure away from dog at nose height, then lower it a tad. 12) "Phoenix, off! Good stand, Phoenix!" 13) "Phoenix, down!" 14) Hand palm downwards, move lure down to lie between dog's forepaws. 15) "Phoenix, off! Good down-stay, Phoenix!" 16) "Phoenix, stand!" 17) Move lure away from dog's muzzle up to nose height. 18) "Phoenix, off! Good stand-stay, Phoenix. Now we'll make the vet and groomer happy!"

as the dog stands, lower the lure to just beneath the dog's chin to entice her to look down; otherwise she will stand and then sit immediately. To prompt the dog to stand from the down position, move the lure half a dog-length upwards and away from the dog, holding the lure at standing nose height from the floor.

Teaching *rollover* is best started from the down position, with the dog lying on one side, or at least with both hind legs stretched out on the same side. Say "Tina, bang!" and move the lure backwards and alongside the dog's muzzle to her elbow (on the side of her outstretched hind legs). Once the dog looks to the side and backwards, very slowly move the lure upwards to the dog's shoulder and backbone. Tickling the dog in the goolies (groin area) often invokes a reflex-raising of the hind leg as an appeasement gesture, which facilitates the tendency to roll over. If you move the lure too quickly and the dog jumps into the standing position, have patience and start again. As soon as the dog rolls onto her back, keep the lure stationary and mesmerize the dog with a relaxing tummy rub.

To teach *rollover-stay* when the dog is standing or moving, say "Tina, bang!" and give the appropriate hand signal (with index finger pointed and thumb cocked in true Sam Spade fashion), then in one fluid movement lure her to first lie down and then rollover-stay as above.

Teaching the dog to *stay* in each of the above four positions becomes a piece of cake after first teaching the dog not to worry at the toy or treat training lure. This is best accomplished by hand feeding dinner kibble. Hold a piece of kibble firmly in your hand and softly instruct "Off!" Ignore any licking and slobbering *for however long the dog worries at the treat*, but say "Take it!" and offer the kibble *the instant* the dog breaks contact with her muzzle. Repeat this a few times, and then up the ante and insist the dog remove her muzzle for one whole second before offering the kibble. Then progressively refine your criteria and have the dog not touch your hand (or treat) for longer and longer periods on each trial, such as for two seconds, four seconds, then six, ten, fifteen, twenty, thirty seconds and so on.

The dog soon learns: (1) worrying at the treat never gets results, whereas (2) noncontact is often rewarded after a variable time lapse.

Teaching *"Off!"* has many useful applications in its own right. Additionally, instructing the dog not to touch a training lure often produces spontaneous and magical stays. Request the dog to stand-stay, for example, and not to touch the lure. At first set your sights on a short two-second stay before rewarding the dog. (Remember, every long journey begins with a single step.) However, on subsequent trials, gradually and progressively increase the length of stay required to receive a reward. In no time at all your dog will stand calmly for a minute or so.

Relevancy Training

Once you have taught the dog what you expect her to do when requested to come, sit, lie down, stand, roll-over and stay, the time is right to teach the dog *why* she should comply with your wishes. The secret is to have many (*many*) extremely short training interludes (two to five seconds each) at numerous (*numerous*) times during the course of the dog's day. Especially work with the dog immediately *before* the dog's good times and *during* the dog's good times. For example, ask your dog to sit and/or lie down each time before opening doors, serving meals, offering treats and tummy rubs; ask the dog to perform a few controlled doggy push-ups before letting her off leash or throwing a tennis ball; and perhaps request the dog to sit-down-sit-stand-down-stand-rollover before inviting her to cuddle on the couch.

Similarly, request the dog to sit many times during play or on walks, and in no time at all the dog will be only too pleased to follow your instructions because she has learned that a compliant response heralds all sorts of goodies. Basically all you are trying to teach the dog is how to say please: "Please throw the tennis ball. Please may I snuggle on the couch."

119

Remember, it is important to keep training interludes short and to have many short sessions each and every day. The shortest (and most useful) session comprises asking the dog to sit and then go play during a play session. When trained this way, your dog will soon associate training with good times. In fact, the dog may be unable to distinguish between training and good times and, indeed, there should be no distinction. The warped concept that training involves forcing the dog to comply and/or dominating her will is totally at odds with the picture of a truly well-trained dog. In reality, enjoying a game of training with a dog is no different from enjoying a game of backgammon or tennis with a friend; and walking with a dog should be no different from strolling with a spouse, or with buddies on the golf course.

Walk by Your Side

Many people attempt to teach a dog to heel by putting her on a leash and physically correcting the dog when she makes mistakes. There are a number of things seriously wrong with this approach, the first being that most people do not want precision heeling; rather, they simply want the dog to follow or walk by their side. Second, when physically restrained during "training," even though the dog may grudgingly mope by your side when "handcuffed" on leash, let's see what happens when she is off leash. History! The dog is in the next county because she never enjoyed walking with you on leash and you have no control over her off leash. So let's just teach the dog off leash from the outset to *want* to walk with us. Third, if the dog has not been trained to heel, it is a trifle hasty to think about punishing the poor dog for making mistakes and breaking heeling rules she didn't even know existed. This is simply not fair! Surely, if the dog had been adequately taught how to heel, she would seldom make mistakes and hence there would be no need to correct the dog. Remember, each mistake and each correction (punishment) advertise the trainer's inadequacy, not the dog's. The dog is not stubborn, she is not stupid and she is not bad. Even if she were, she would still require training, so let's train her properly.

Let's teach the dog to *enjoy* following us and to *want* to walk by our side off leash. Then it will be easier to teach high-precision off-leash heeling patterns if desired. Before going on outdoor walks, it is necessary to teach the dog not to pull. Then it becomes easy to teach on-leash walking and heeling because the dog already wants to walk with you, she is familiar with the desired walking and heeling positions and she knows not to pull.

FOLLOWING

Start by training your dog to follow you. Many puppies will follow if you simply walk away from them and maybe click your fingers or chuckle. Adult dogs may require additional enticement to stimulate them to follow, such as a training lure or, at the very least, a lively trainer. To teach the dog to follow: (1) keep walking and (2) walk away from the dog. If the dog attempts to lead or lag, change pace; slow down if the dog forges too far ahead, but speed up if she lags too far behind. Say "Steady!" or "Easy!" each time before you slow down and "Quickly!" or "Hustle!" each time before you speed up, and the dog will learn to change pace on cue. If the dog lags or leads too far, or if she wanders right or left, simply walk quickly in the opposite direction and maybe even run away from the dog and hide.

Practicing is a lot of fun; you can set up a course in your home, yard or park to do this. Indoors, entice the dog to follow upstairs, into a bedroom, into the bathroom, downstairs, around the living room couch, zigzagging between dining room chairs and into the kitchen for dinner. Outdoors, get the dog to follow around park benches, trees, shrubs and along walkways and lines in the grass. (For safety outdoors, it is advisable to attach a long line on the dog, but never exert corrective tension on the line.)

Enjoying Your
Dog

Remember, following has a lot to do with attitude—*your* attitude! Most probably your dog will *not* want to follow Mr. Grumpy Troll with the personality of wilted lettuce. Lighten up—walk with a jaunty step, whistle a happy tune, sing, skip and tell jokes to your dog and she will be right there by your side.

BY YOUR SIDE

It is smart to train the dog to walk close on one side or the other—either side will do, your choice. When walking, jogging or cycling, it is generally bad news to have the dog suddenly cut in front of you. In fact, I train my dogs to walk "By my side" and "Other side"—both very useful instructions. It is possible to position the dog fairly accurately by looking to the appropriate side and clicking your fingers or slapping your thigh on that side. A precise positioning may be attained by holding a training lure, such as a chew toy, tennis ball or food treat. Stop and stand still several times throughout the walk, just as you would when window shopping or meeting a friend. Use the lure to make sure the dog slows down and stays close whenever you stop.

When teaching the dog to heel, we generally want her to sit in heel position when we stop. Teach heel

Using a toy to teach sit-heel-sit sequences: 1) "Phoenix, sit!" Standing still, move lure up and back over dog's muzzle . . . 2) to position dog sitting in heel position on your left side. 3) Say "Phoenix, heel!" and walk ahead, wagging lure in left hand. Change lure to right hand in preparation for sit signal. Say "Sit" and then . . .

position at the standstill and the dog will learn that the default heel position is sitting by your side (left or right—your choice, unless you wish to compete in obedience trials, in which case the dog must heel on the left).

Several times a day, stand up and call your dog to come and sit in heel position—"Tina, heel!" For example, instruct the dog to come to heel each time there are commercials on TV, or each time you turn a page of a novel, and the dog will get it in a single evening.

Practice straight-line heeling and turns separately. With the dog sitting at heel, teach her to turn in place. After each quarter-turn, half-turn or full turn in place, lure the dog to sit at heel. Now it's time for short straight-line heeling sequences, no more than a few steps at a time. Always think of heeling in terms of sit-heel-sit sequences—start and end with the dog in position and do your best to keep her there when moving. Progressively increase the number of steps in each sequence. When the dog remains close for 20 yards of straight-line heeling, it is time to add a few turns and then sign up for a happy-heeling obedience class to get some advice from the experts.

4) use hand signal to lure dog to sit as you stop. Eventually, dog will sit automatically at heel whenever you stop. 5) "Good dog!"

No Pulling on Leash

You can start teaching your dog not to pull on leash anywhere—in front of the television or outdoors—but regardless of location, you must not take a single step with tension in the leash. For a reason known only to dogs, even just a couple of paces of pulling on leash is intrinsically motivating and diabolically rewarding. Instead, attach the leash to the dog's collar, grasp the other end firmly with both hands held close to your chest, and stand still—do not budge an inch. Have somebody watch you with a stopwatch to time your progress, or else you will never believe this will work and so you will not even try the exercise, and your shoulder and the dog's neck will be traumatized for years to come.

Stand still and wait for the dog to stop pulling, and to sit and/or lie down. All dogs stop pulling and sit eventually. Most take only a couple of minutes; the all-time record is 22½ minutes. Time how long it takes. Gently praise the dog when she stops pulling, and as soon as she sits, enthusiastically praise the dog and take just one step forward, then immediately stand still. This single step usually demonstrates the ballistic reinforcing nature of pulling on leash; most dogs explode to the end of the leash, so be prepared for the strain. Stand firm and wait for the dog to sit again. Repeat this half a dozen times and you will probably notice a progressive reduction in the force of the dog's one-step explosions and a radical reduction in the time it takes for the dog to sit each time.

As the dog learns "Sit we go" and "Pull we stop," she will begin to walk forward calmly with each single step and automatically sit when you stop. Now try two steps before you stop. Wooooooo! Scary! When the dog has mastered two steps at a time, try for three. After each success, progressively increase the number of steps in the sequence: try four steps and then six, eight, ten and twenty steps before stopping. Congratulations! You are now walking the dog on leash.

Whenever walking with the dog (off leash or on leash), make sure you stop periodically to practice a few position commands and stays before instructing the dog to "Walk on!" (Remember, you want the dog to be compliant everywhere, not just in the kitchen when her dinner is at hand.) For example, stopping every 25 yards to briefly train the dog amounts to over 200 training interludes within a single 3-mile stroll. And each training session is in a different location. You will not believe the improvement within just the first mile of the first walk.

To put it another way, integrating training into a walk offers 200 separate opportunities to use the continuance of the walk as a reward to reinforce the dog's education. Moreover, some training interludes may comprise continuing education for the dog's walking skills: Alternate short periods of the dog walking calmly by your side with periods when the dog is allowed to sniff and investigate the environment. Now sniffing odors on the grass and meeting other dogs become rewards which reinforce the dog's calm and mannerly demeanor. Good Lord! Whatever next? Many enjoyable walks together of course. Happy trails!

THE IMPORTANCE OF TRICKS

Nothing will improve a dog's quality of life better than having a few tricks under her belt. Teaching any trick expands the dog's vocabulary, which facilitates communication and improves the owner's control. Also, specific tricks help prevent and resolve specific behavior problems. For example, by teaching the dog to fetch her toys, the dog learns carrying a toy makes the owner happy and, therefore, will be more likely to chew her toy than other inappropriate items.

More important, teaching tricks prompts owners to lighten up and train with a sunny disposition. Really, tricks should be no different from any other behaviors we put on cue. But they are. When teaching tricks, owners have a much sweeter attitude, which in turn motivates the dog and improves her willingness to comply. The dog feels tricks are a blast, but formal commands are a drag. In fact, tricks are so enjoyable, they may be used as rewards in training by asking the dog to come, sit and down-stay and then rollover for a tummy rub. Go on, try it: Crack a smile and even giggle when the dog promptly and willingly lies down and stays.

Most important, performing tricks prompts onlookers to smile and gig- gle. Many people are scared of dogs, especially large ones. And noth- ing can be more off-putting for a dog than to be constantly confronted by strangers who don't like her because of her size or the way she looks. Uneasy people put the dog on edge, causing her to back off and bark, only frightening people all the more. And so a vicious circle devel- ops, with the people's fear fueling the dog's fear *and vice versa*. Instead, tie a pink ribbon to your dog's collar and practice all sorts of tricks on walks and in the park, and you will be pleasantly amazed how it changes people's attitudes toward your friendly dog. The dog's reper- toire of tricks is limited only by the trainer's imagination. Below I have described three of my favorites:

SPEAK AND SHUSH

The training sequence involved in teaching a dog to bark on request is no different from that used when training any behavior on cue: request—lure—response—reward. As always, the secret of success lies in finding an effective lure. If the dog always barks at the doorbell, for example, say "Rover, speak!", have an accomplice ring the doorbell, then reward the dog for barking. After a few woofs, ask Rover to "Shush!", waggle a food treat under her nose (to entice her to sniff and thus to shush), praise her when quiet and eventually offer the treat as a reward. Alternate "Speak" and "Shush," progressively increasing the length of shush-time between each barking bout.

PLAY BOW

With the dog standing, say "Bow!" and lower the food lure (palm upwards) to rest between the dog's forepaws. Praise as the dog lowers

her forequarters and sternum to the ground (as when teaching the down), but then lure the dog to stand and offer the treat. On successive trials, gradually increase the length of time the dog is required to remain in the play bow posture in order to gain a food reward. If the dog's rear end collapses into a down, say nothing and offer no reward; simply start over.

BE A BEAR

With the dog sitting backed into a corner to prevent her from toppling over backwards, say "Be a bear!" With bent paw and palm down, raise a lure upwards and backwards along the top of the dog's muzzle. Praise the dog when she sits up on her haunches and offer the treat as a reward. To prevent the dog from standing on her hind legs, keep the lure closer to the dog's muzzle. On each trial, progressively increase the length of time the dog is required to sit up to receive a food reward. Since lure-reward training is so easy, teach the dog to stand and walk on her hind legs as well!

Teaching "Be a Bear"

Getting **Active** with your Dog

by Bardi McLennan

Once you and your dog have graduated from basic obedience training and are beginning to work together as a team, you can take part in the growing world of dog activities. There are so many fun things to do with your dog! Just remember, people and dogs don't always learn at the same pace, so don't be upset if you (or your dog) need more than two basic training courses before your team becomes operational. Even smart dogs don't go straight to college from kindergarten!

Just as there are events geared to certain types of dogs, so there are ones that are more appealing to certain types of people. In some

128

activities, you give the commands and your dog does the work (upland game hunting is one example), while in others, such as agility, you'll both get a workout. You may want to aim for prestigious titles to add to your dog's name, or you may want nothing more than the sheer enjoyment of being around other people and their dogs. Passive or active, participation has its own rewards.

Consider your dog's physical capabilities when looking into any of the canine activities. It's easy to see that a Basset Hound is not built for the racetrack, nor would a Chihuahua be the breed of choice for pulling a sled. A loyal dog will attempt almost anything you ask him to do, so it is up to you to know your

All dogs seem to love playing flyball.

dog's limitations. A dog must be physically sound in order to compete at any level in athletic activities, and being mentally sound is a definite plus. Advanced age, however, may not be a deterrent. Many dogs still hunt and herd at ten or twelve years of age. It's entirely possible for dogs to be "fit at 50." Take your dog for a checkup, explain to your vet the type of activity you have in mind and be guided by his or her findings.

You needn't be restricted to breed-specific sports if it's only fun you're after. Certain AKC activities are limited to designated breeds; however, as each new trial, test or sport has grown in popularity, so has the variety of breeds encouraged to participate at a fun level.

But don't shortchange your fun, or that of your dog, by thinking only of the basic function of her breed. Once a dog has learned how to learn, she can be taught to do just about anything as long as the size of the dog is right for the job and you both think it is fun and rewarding. In other words, you are a team.

129

To get involved in any of the activities detailed in this chapter, look for the names and addresses of the organizations that sponsor them in Chapter 13. You can also ask your breeder or a local dog trainer for contacts.

You can compete in obedience trials with a well trained dog.

Official American Kennel Club Activities

The following tests and trials are some of the events sanctioned by the AKC and sponsored by various dog clubs. Your dog's expertise will be rewarded with impressive titles. You can participate just for fun, or be competitive and go for those awards.

OBEDIENCE

Training classes begin with pups as young as three months of age in kindergarten puppy training, then advance to pre-novice (all exercises on lead) and go on to novice, which is where you'll start off-lead work. In obedience classes dogs learn to sit, stay, heel and come through a variety of exercises. Once you've got the basics down, you can enter obedience trials and work toward earning your dog's first degree, a C.D. (Companion Dog).

The next level is called "Open," in which jumps and retrieves perk up the dog's interest. Passing grades in competition at this level earn a C.D.X. (Companion Dog Excellent). Beyond that lies the goal of the most ambitious—Utility (U.D. and even U.D.X. or OTCh, an Obedience Champion).

AGILITY

All dogs can participate in the latest canine sport to have gained worldwide popularity for its fun and excitement, agility. It began in England as a canine version of horse show-jumping, but because dogs are more agile and able to perform on verbal commands, extra feats were added such as climbing, balancing and racing through tunnels or in and out of weave poles. Many of the obstacles (regulation or homemade) can be set up in your own backyard. If the agility bug bites, you could end up in international competition!

For starters, your dog should be obedience trained, even though, in the beginning, the lessons may all be taught on lead. Once the dog understands the commands (and you do, too), it's as easy as guiding the dog over a prescribed course, one obstacle at a time. In competition, the race is against the clock, so wear your running shoes! The dog starts with 200 points and the judge deducts for infractions and misadventures along the way.

All dogs seem to love agility and respond to it as if they were being turned loose in a playground paradise. Your dog's enthusiasm will be contagious; agility turns into great fun for dog and owner.

Field Trials and Hunting Tests

There are field trials and hunting tests for the sporting breeds—retrievers, spaniels and pointing breeds, and for some hounds—Bassets, Beagles and Dachshunds. Field trials are competitive events that test a dog's ability to perform the functions for which she was bred. Hunting tests, which are open to retrievers,

TITLES AWARDED BY THE AKC

Conformation: Ch. (Champion)

Obedience: CD (Companion Dog); CDX (Companion Dog Excellent); UD (Utility Dog); UDX (Utility Dog Excellent); OTCh. (Obedience Trial Champion)

Field: JH (Junior Hunter); SH (Senior Hunter); MH (Master Hunter); AFCh. (Amateur Field Champion); FCh. (Field Champion)

Lure Coursing: JC (Junior Courser); SC (Senior Courser)

Herding: HT (Herding Tested); PT (Pre-Trial Tested); HS (Herding Started); HI (Herding Intermediate); HX (Herding Excellent); HCh. (Herding Champion)

Tracking: TD (Tracking Dog); TDX (Tracking Dog Excellent)

Agility: NAD (Novice Agility); OAD (Open Agility); ADX (Agility Excellent); MAX (Master Agility)

Earthdog Tests: JE (Junior Earthdog); SE (Senior Earthdog); ME (Master Earthdog)

Canine Good Citizen: CGC

Combination: DC (Dual Champion—Ch. and Fch.); TC (Triple Champion—Ch., Fch., and OTch.)

spaniels and pointing breeds only, are noncompetitive and are a means of judging the dog's ability as well as that of the handler.

Hunting is a very large and complex part of canine sports, and if you own one of the breeds that hunts, the events are a great treat for your dog and you. He gets to do what he was bred for, and you get to work with him and watch him do it. You'll be proud of and amazed at what your dog can do.

Retrievers and other sporting breeds get to do what they're bred to in hunting tests.

Fortunately, the AKC publishes a series of booklets on these events, which outline the rules and regulations and include a glossary of the sometimes complicated terms. The AKC also publishes newsletters for field trialers and hunting test enthusiasts. The United Kennel Club (UKC) also has informative materials for the hunter and his dog.

HERDING TESTS AND TRIALS

Herding, like hunting, dates back to the first known uses man made of dogs. The interest in herding today is widespread, and if you own a herding breed, you can join in the activity. Herding dogs are tested for their natural skills to keep a flock of ducks, sheep or cattle together. If your dog shows potential, you can start at the testing level, where your dog can earn a title for showing an inherent herding ability. With training you can advance to the trial level, where your dog should be capable of controlling even difficult livestock in diverse situations.

LURE COURSING

The AKC Tests and Trials for Lure Coursing are open to traditional sighthounds—Greyhounds, Whippets,

Borzoi, Salukis, Afghan Hounds, Ibizan Hounds and Scottish Deerhounds—as well as to Basenjis and Rhodesian Ridgebacks. Hounds are judged on overall ability, follow, speed, agility and endurance. This is possibly the most exciting of the trials for spectators, because the speed and agility of the dogs is awesome to watch as they chase the lure (or "course") in heats of two or three dogs at a time.

TRACKING

Tracking is another activity in which almost any dog can compete because every dog that sniffs the ground when taken outdoors is, in fact, tracking. The hard part comes when the rules as to what, when and where the dog tracks are determined by a person, not the dog! Tracking tests cover a large area of fields, woods and roads. The tracks are laid hours before the dogs go to work on them, and include "tricks" like cross-tracks and sharp turns. If you're interested in search-and-rescue work, this is the place to start.

This tracking dog is hot on the trail.

EARTHDOG TESTS FOR SMALL TERRIERS AND DACHSHUNDS

These tests are open to Australian, Bedlington, Border, Cairn, Dandie Dinmont, Smooth and Wire Fox, Lakeland, Norfolk, Norwich, Scottish, Sealyham, Skye, Welsh and West Highland White Terriers as well as Dachshunds. The dogs need no prior training for this terrier sport. There is a qualifying test on the day of the event, so dog and handler learn the rules on the spot. These tests, or "digs," sometimes end with informal races in the late afternoon.

133

Here are some of the extracurricular obedience and racing activities that are not regulated by the AKC or UKC, but are generally run by clubs or a group of dog fanciers and are often open to all.

Canine Freestyle This activity is something new on the scene and is variously likened to dancing, dressage or ice skating. It is meant to show the athleticism of the dog, but also requires showmanship on the part of the dog's handler. If you and your dog like to ham it up for friends, you might want to look into freestyle.

Lure coursing lets sighthounds do what they do best—run!

Scent Hurdle Racing Scent hurdle racing is purely a fun activity sponsored by obedience clubs with members forming competing teams. The height of the hurdles is based on the size of the shortest dog on the team. On a signal, one team dog is released on each of two side-by-side courses and must clear every hurdle before picking up its own dumbbell from a platform and returning over the jumps to the handler. As each dog returns, the next on that team is sent. Of course, that is what the dogs are supposed to do. When the dogs improvise (going under or around the hurdles, stealing another dog's dumbbell, and so forth), it no doubt frustrates the handlers, but just adds to the fun for everyone else.

Flyball This type of racing is similar, but after negotiating the four hurdles, the dog comes to a flyball box, steps on a lever that releases a tennis ball into the air, catches the ball and returns over the hurdles to the starting point. This game also becomes extremely fun for spectators because the dogs sometimes cheat by catching a ball released by the dog in the next lane. Three titles can be earned—Flyball Dog (F.D.), Flyball Dog Excellent (F.D.X.) and Flyball Dog Champion (Fb.D.Ch.)—all awarded by the North American Flyball Association, Inc.

Dogsledding The name conjures up the Rocky Mountains or the frigid North, but you can find dogsled clubs in such unlikely spots as Maryland, North Carolina and Virginia! Dogsledding is primarily for the Nordic breeds such as the Alaskan Malamutes, Siberian Huskies and Samoyeds, but other breeds can try. There are some practical backyard applications to this sport, too. With parental supervision, almost any strong dog could pull a child's sled.

Coming over the A-frame on an agility course.

These are just some of the many recreational ways you can get to know and understand your multifaceted dog better and have fun doing it.

Your Dog
and your
Family

by Bardi McLennan

Adding a dog automatically increases your family by one, no matter whether you live alone in an apartment or are part of a mother, father and six kids household. The single-person family is fair game for numerous and varied canine misconceptions as to who is dog and who pays the bills, whereas a dog in a houseful of children will consider himself to be just one of the gang, littermates all. One dog and one child may give a dog reason to believe they are both kids or both dogs.

Either interpretation requires parental supervision and sometimes speedy intervention.

As soon as one paw goes through the door into your home, Rufus (or Rufina) has to make many adjustments to become a part of your

136

family. Your job is to make him fit in as painlessly as possible. An older dog may have some frame of reference from past experience, but to a 10-week-old puppy, everything is brand new: people, furniture, stairs, when and where people eat, sleep or watch TV, his own place and everyone else's space, smells, sounds, outdoors—everything!

Puppies, and newly acquired dogs of any age, do not need what we think of as "freedom." If you leave a new dog or puppy loose in the house, you will almost certainly return to chaotic destruction and the dog will forever after equate your homecoming with a time of punishment to be dreaded. It is unfair to give your dog what amounts to "freedom to get into trouble." Instead, confine him to a crate for brief periods of your absence (up to three or four hours) and, for the long haul, a workday for example, confine him to one untrashable area with his own toys, a bowl of water and a radio left on (low) in another room.

Lots of pets get along with each other just fine.

For the first few days, when not confined, put Rufus on a long leash tied to your wrist or waist. This umbilical cord method enables the dog to learn all about you from your body language and voice, and to learn by his own actions which things in the house are NO! and which ones are rewarded by "Good dog." House-training will be easier with the pup always by your side. Speaking of which, accidents do happen. That goal of "completely housetrained" takes up to a year, or the length of time it takes the pup to mature.

The All-Adult Family

Most dogs in an adults-only household today are likely to be latchkey pets, with no one home all day but the dog. When you return after a tough day on the job, the dog can and should be your relaxation therapy. But going home can instead be a daily frustration.

Separation anxiety is a very common problem for the dog in a working household. It may begin with whines and barks of loneliness, but it will soon escalate into a frenzied destruction derby. That is why it is so important to set aside the time to teach a dog to relax when left alone in his confined area and to understand that he can trust you to return.

Let the dog get used to your work schedule in easy stages. Confine him to one room and go in and out of that room over and over again. Be casual about it. No physical, voice or eye contact. When the pup no longer even notices your comings and goings, leave the house for varying lengths of time, returning to stay home for a few minutes and gradually increasing the time away. This training can take days, but the dog is learning that you haven't left him forever and that he can trust you.

Any time you leave the dog, but especially during this training period, be casual about your departure. No anxiety-building fond farewells. Just "Bye" and go! Remember the "Good dog" when you return to find everything more or less as you left it.

If things are a mess (or even a disaster) when you return, greet the dog, take him outside to eliminate, and then put him in his crate while you clean up. Rant and rave in the shower! *Do not* punish the dog. You were not there when it happened, and the rule is: Only punish as you catch the dog in the act of wrongdoing. Obviously, it makes sense to get your latchkey puppy when you'll have a week or two to spend on these training essentials.

Family weekend activities should include Rufus whenever possible. Depending on the pup's age, now is the time for a long walk in the park, playtime in the backyard, a hike in the woods. Socializing is as important as health care, good food and physical exercise, so visiting Aunt Emma or Uncle Harry and the next-door neighbor's dog or cat is essential to developing an out-going, friendly temperament in your pet.

If you are a single adult, socializing Rufus at home and away will prevent him from becoming overly protective of you (or just overly attached) and will also prevent such behavioral problems as dominance or fear of strangers.

Babies

Whether already here or on the way, babies figure larger than life in the eyes of a dog. If the dog is there first, let him in on all your baby preparations in the house. When baby arrives, let Rufus sniff any item of clothing that has been on the baby before Junior comes home. Then let Mom greet the dog first before introducing the new family member. Hold the baby down for the dog to see and sniff, but make sure some-one's holding the dog on lead in case of any sudden moves. Don't play keep-away or tease the dog with the baby, which only invites undesirable jump-ing up.

The dog and the baby are "family," and for starters can be treated almost as equals. Things rapidly change, however, espe-cially when baby takes to creeping around on all fours on the dog's turf or, better yet, has yummy pudding all over her face and hands! That's when a lot of things in the dog's and baby's lives become more separate than equal.

Dogs are perfect confidants.

Toddlers make terrible dog owners, but if you can't avoid the combination, use patient discipline (that is, positive teaching rather than punishment), and use timc-outs before you run out of patience.

A dog and a baby (or toddler, or an assertive young child) should never be left alone together. Take the dog with you or confine him. With a baby or youngsters in the house, you'll have plenty of use for that wonderful canine safety device called a crate!

Young Children

Any dog in a house with kids will behave pretty much as the kids do, good or bad. But even good dogs and good children can get into trouble when play becomes rowdy and active.

Legs bobbing up and down, shrill voices screeching, a ball hurtling overhead, all add up to exuberant frustration for a dog who's just trying to be part of the gang. In a pack of puppies, any legs or toys being chased would be caught by a set of teeth, and all the pups involved would understand that is how the game is played. Kids do not understand this, nor do parents tolerate it. Bring Rufus indoors before you have reason to regret it. This is time-out, not a punishment.

Teach children how to play nicely with a puppy.

You can explain the situation to the children and tell them they must play quieter games until the puppy learns not to grab them with his mouth. Unfortunately, you can't explain it that easily to the dog. With adult supervision, they will learn how to play together.

Young children love to tease. Sticking their faces or wiggling their hands or fingers in the dog's face is teasing. To another person it might be just annoying, but it is threatening to a dog. There's another difference: We can make the child stop by an explanation, but the only way a dog can stop it is with a warning growl and then with teeth. Teasing is the major cause of children being bitten by their pets. Treat it seriously.

Older Children

The best age for a child to get a first dog is between the ages of 8 and 12. That's when kids are able to accept some real responsibility for their pet. Even so, take the child's vow of "I will never *ever* forget to feed (brush, walk, etc.) the dog" for what it's worth: a child's good intention at that moment. Most kids today have extra lessons, soccer practice, Little League, ballet, and so forth piled on top of school schedules. There will be many times when Mom will have to come to the dog's rescue. "I walked the dog for you so you can set the table for me" is one way to get around a missed appointment without laying on blame or guilt.

Kids in this age group make excellent obedience trainers because they are into the teaching/learning process themselves and they lack the self-consciousness of adults. Attending a dog show is something the whole family can enjoy, and watching Junior Showmanship may catch the eye of the kids. Older children can begin to get involved in many of the recreational activities that were reviewed in the previous chapter. Some of the agility obstacles, for example, can be set up in the backyard as a family project (with an adult making sure all the equipment is safe and secure for the dog).

Older kids are also beginning to look to the future, and may envision themselves as veterinarians or trainers or show dog handlers or writers of the next Lassie best-seller. Dogs are perfect confidants for these dreams. They won't tell a soul.

Other Pets

Introduce all pets tactfully. In a dog/cat situation, hold the dog, not the cat. Let two dogs meet on neutral turf—a stroll in the park or a walk down the street—with both on loose leads to permit all the normal canine ways of saying hello, including routine sniffing, circling, more sniffing, and so on. Small creatures such as hamsters, chinchillas or mice must be kept safe from their natural predators (dogs and cats).

Festive Family Occasions

Parties are great for people, but not necessarily for puppies. Until all the guests have arrived, put the dog in his crate or in a room where he won't be disturbed. A socialized dog can join the fun later as long as he's not underfoot, annoying guests or into the hors d'oeuvres.

There are a few dangers to consider, too. Doors opening and closing can allow a puppy to slip out unnoticed in the confusion, and you'll be organizing a search party instead of playing host or hostess. Party food and buffet service are not for dogs. Let Rufus party in his crate with a nice big dog biscuit.

At Christmas time, not only are tree decorations dangerous and breakable (and perhaps family heirlooms), but extreme caution should be taken with the lights, cords and outlets for the tree lights and any other festive lighting. Occasionally a dog lifts a leg, ignoring the fact that the tree is indoors. To avoid this, use a canine repellent, made for gardens, on the tree. Or keep him out of the tree room unless supervised. And whatever you do, *don't* invite trouble by hanging his toys on the tree!

Car Travel

Before you plan a vacation by car or RV with Rufus, be sure he enjoys car travel. Nothing spoils a holiday quicker than a carsick dog! Work within the dog's comfort level. Get in the car with the dog in his crate or attached to a canine car safety belt and just sit there until he relaxes. That's all. Next time, get in the car, turn on the engine and go nowhere. Just sit. When that is okay, turn on the engine and go around the block. Now you can go for a ride and include a stop where you get out, leaving the dog for a minute or two.

On a warm day, always park in the shade and leave windows open several inches. And return quickly. It only takes 10 minutes for a car to become an overheated steel death trap.

Motel or Pet Motel?

Not all motels or hotels accept pets, but you have a much better choice today than even a few years ago. To find a dog-friendly lodging, look at *On the Road Again With Man's Best Friend*, a series of directories that detail bed and breakfasts, inns, family resorts and other hotels/motels. Some places require a refundable deposit to cover any damage incurred by the dog. More B&Bs accept pets now, but some restrict the size.

If taking Rufus with you is not feasible, check out boarding kennels in your area. Your veterinarian may offer this service, or recommend a kennel or two he or she is familiar with. Go see the facilities for yourself, ask about exercise, diet, housing, and so on. Or, if you'd rather have Rufus stay home, look into bonded petsitters, many of whom will also bring in the mail and water your plants.

chapter 11

Your Dog
and your
Community

by Bardi McLennan

Step outside your home with your dog and you are no longer just family, you are both part of your community. This is when the phrase "responsible pet ownership" takes on serious implications. For starters, it means you pick up after your dog—not just occasionally, but every time your dog eliminates away from home. That means you have joined the Plastic Baggy Brigade! You always have plastic sandwich bags in your pocket and several in the car. It means you teach your kids how to use them, too. If you think this is "yucky," just imagine what

the person (a non-doggy person) who inadvertently steps in the mess thinks!

Your responsibility extends to your neighbors: To their ears (no annoying barking); to their property (their garbage, their lawn, their flower beds, their cat— especially their cat); to their kids (on bikes, at play); to their kids' toys and sports equipment.

There are numerous dog-related laws, ranging from simple dog licensing and leash laws to those holding you liable for any physical injury or property damage done by your dog. These laws are in place to protect everyone in the community, including you and your dog. There are town ordinances and state laws which are by no means the same in all towns or all states. Ignorance of the law won't get you off the hook. The time to find out what the laws are where you live is now.

Be sure your dog's license is current. This is not just a good local ordinance, it can make the difference between finding your lost dog or not.

Dressing your dog up makes him appealing to strangers.

Many states now require proof of rabies vaccination and that the dog has been spayed or neutered before issuing a license. At the same time, keep up the dog's annual immunizations.

Never let your dog run loose in the neighborhood. This will not only keep you on the right side of the leash law, it's the outdoor version of the rule about not giving your dog "freedom to get into trouble."

Good Canine Citizen

Sometimes it's hard for a dog's owner to assess whether or not the dog is sufficiently socialized to be accepted by the community at large. Does Rufus or Rufina display good, controlled behavior in public? The AKC's Canine Good Citizen program is available through many dog organizations. If your dog passes the test, the title "CGC" is earned.

The overall purpose is to turn your dog into a good neighbor and to teach you about your responsibility to your community as a dog owner. Here are the ten things your dog must do willingly:

1. Accept a stranger stopping to chat with you.
2. Sit and be petted by a stranger.
3. Allow a stranger to handle him or her as a groomer or veterinarian would.
4. Walk nicely on a loose lead.
5. Walk calmly through a crowd.
6. Sit and down on command, then stay in a sit or down position while you walk away.
7. Come when called.
8. Casually greet another dog.
9. React confidently to distractions.
10. Accept being left alone with someone other than you and not become overly agitated or nervous.

Schools and Dogs

Schools are getting involved with pet ownership on an educational level. It has been proven that children who are kind to animals are humane in their attitude toward other people as adults.

A dog is a child's best friend, and so children are often primary pet owners, if not the primary caregivers. Unfortunately, they are also the ones most often bitten by dogs. This occurs due to a lack of understanding that pets, no matter how sweet, cuddly and loving, are still animals. Schools, along with parents, dog clubs, dog fanciers and the AKC, are working to change all that with video programs for children not only in grade school, but in the nursery school and pre-kindergarten age group. Teaching youngsters how to be responsible dog owners is important community work. When your dog has a CGC, volunteer to take part in an educational classroom event put on by your dog club.

Boy Scout Merit Badge

A Merit Badge for Dog Care can be earned by any Boy
Scout ages 11 to 18. The requirements are not easy, but
amount to a complete course in responsible dog care
and general ownership. Here are just a few of the
things a Scout must do to earn that badge:

> Point out ten parts of the dog using the correct
> names.

> Give a report (signed by parent or guardian) on
> your care of the dog (feeding, food used, housing,
> exercising, grooming and bathing), plus what has
> been done to keep the dog healthy.

> Explain the right way to obedience train a dog,
> and demonstrate three comments.

> Several of the requirements have to do with health
> care, including first aid, handling a hurt dog, and
> the dangers of home treatment for a serious
> ailment.

> The final requirement is to know the local laws
> and ordinances involving dogs.

There are similar programs for Girl Scouts and 4-H
members.

Local Clubs

Local dog clubs are no longer in existence just to put
on a yearly dog show. Today, they are apt to be the hub
of the community's involvement with pets. Dog clubs
conduct educational forums with big-name speakers,
stage demonstrations of canine talent in a busy mall
and take dogs of various breeds to schools for classroom discussion.

The quickest way to feel accepted as a member in a
club is to volunteer your services! Offer to help with
something—anything—and watch your popularity
(and your interest) grow.

Therapy Dogs

Once your dog has earned that essential CGC and reliably demonstrates a steady, calm temperament, you could look into what therapy dogs are doing in your area.

Therapy dogs go with their owners to visit patients at hospitals or nursing homes, generally remaining on leash but able to coax a pat from a stiffened hand, a smile from a blank face, a few words from sealed lips or a hug from someone in need of love.

Nursing homes cover a wide range of patient care. Some specialize in care of the elderly, some in the treatment of specific illnesses, some in physical therapy. Children's facilities also welcome visits from trained therapy dogs for boosting morale in their pediatric patients. Hospice care for the terminally ill and the at-home care of AIDS patients are other areas where this canine visiting is desperately needed. Therapy dog training comes first.

Your dog can make a difference in lots of lives.

There is a lot more involved than just taking your nice friendly pooch to someone's bedside. Doing therapy dog work involves your own emotional stability as well as that of your dog. But once you have met all the requirements for this work, making the rounds once a week or once a month with your therapy dog is possibly the most rewarding of all community activities.

Disaster Aid

This community service is definitely not for everyone, partly because it is time-consuming. The initial training is rigorous, and there can be no let-up in the continuing workouts, because members are on call 24 hours a day to go wherever they are needed at a moment's notice. But if you think you would like to be able to assist in a disaster, look into search-and-rescue work. The network of search-and-rescue volunteers is worldwide, and all members of the American Rescue Dog Association (ARDA) who are qualified to do this work are volunteers who train and maintain their own dogs.

Physical Aid

Most people are familiar with Seeing Eye dogs, which serve as blind people's eyes, but not with all the other work that dogs are trained to do to assist the disabled. Dogs are also specially trained to pull wheelchairs, carry school books, pick up dropped objects, open and close doors. Some also are ears for the deaf. All these assistance-trained dogs, by the way, are allowed anywhere "No Pet" signs exist (as are therapy dogs when

properly identified). Getting started in any of this fascinating work requires a background in dog training and canine behavior, but there are also volunteer jobs ranging from answering the phone to cleaning out kennels to providing a foster home for a puppy. You have only to ask.

Making the rounds with your therapy dog can be very rewarding.

part four

Beyond
the
Basics

chapter 12

Recommended Reading

Books

ABOUT HEALTH CARE

Ackerman, Lowell. *Guide to Skin and Haircoat Problems in Dogs.* Loveland, Colo.: Alpine Publications, 1994.

Alderton, David. *The Dog Care Manual.* Hauppauge, N.Y.: Barron's Educational Series, Inc., 1986.

American Kennel Club. *American Kennel Club Dog Care and Training.* New York: Howell Book House, 1991.

Bamberger, Michelle, DVM. *Help! The Quick Guide to First Aid for Your Dog.* New York: Howell Book House, 1995.

Carlson, Delbert, DVM, and James Giffin, MD. *Dog Owner's Home Veterinary Handbook.* New York: Howell Book House, 1992.

DeBitetto, James, DVM, and Sarah Hodgson. *You & Your Puppy.* New York: Howell Book House, 1995.

Humphries, Jim, DVM. *Dr. Jim's Animal Clinic for Dogs.* New York: Howell Book House, 1994.

McGinnis, Terri. *The Well Dog Book.* New York: Random House, 1991.

Pitcairn, Richard and Susan. *Natural Health for Dogs.* Emmaus, Pa.: Rodale Press, 1982.

ABOUT DOG SHOWS

Hall, Lynn. *Dog Showing for Beginners.* New York: Howell Book House, 1994.

Nichols, Virginia Tuck. *How to Show Your Own Dog.* Neptune, N. J.: TFH, 1970.

Vanacore, Connie. *Dog Showing, An Owner's Guide.* New York: Howell Book House, 1990.

ABOUT TRAINING

Ammen, Amy. *Training in No Time.* New York: Howell Book House, 1995.

Baer, Ted. *Communicating With Your Dog.* Hauppauge, N.Y.: Barron's Educational Series, Inc., 1989.

Benjamin, Carol Lea. *Dog Problems.* New York: Howell Book House, 1989.

Benjamin, Carol Lea. *Dog Training for Kids.* New York: Howell Book House, 1988.

Benjamin, Carol Lea. *Mother Knows Best.* New York: Howell Book House, 1985.

Benjamin, Carol Lea. *Surviving Your Dog's Adolescence.* New York: Howell Book House, 1993.

Bohnenkamp, Gwen. *Manners for the Modern Dog.* San Francisco: Perfect Paws, 1990.

Dibra, Bashkim. *Dog Training by Bash.* New York: Dell, 1992.

Dunbar, Ian, PhD, MRCVS. *Dr. Dunbar's Good Little Dog Book*, James & Kenneth Publishers, 2140 Shattuck Ave. #2406, Berkeley, Calif. 94704. (510) 658–8588. Order from the publisher.

Dunbar, Ian, PhD, MRCVS. *How to Teach a New Dog Old Tricks*, James & Kenneth Publishers. Order from the publisher; address above.

Dunbar, Ian, PhD, MRCVS, and Gwen Bohnenkamp. Booklets on *Preventing Aggression; Housetraining; Chewing; Digging; Barking; Socialization; Fearfulness; and Fighting*, James & Kenneth Publishers. Order from the publisher; address above.

Evans, Job Michael. *People, Pooches and Problems.* New York: Howell Book House, 1991.

Kilcommons, Brian and Sarah Wilson. *Good Owners, Great Dogs.* New York: Warner Books, 1992.

McMains, Joel M. *Dog Logic—Companion Obedience.* New York: Howell Book House, 1992.

Rutherford, Clarice and David H. Neil, MRCVS. *How to Raise a Puppy You Can Live With.* Loveland, Colo.: Alpine Publications, 1982.

Volhard, Jack and Melissa Bartlett. *What All Good Dogs Should Know: The Sensible Way to Train.* New York: Howell Book House, 1991.

ABOUT BREEDING

Harris, Beth J. Finder. *Breeding a Litter, The Complete Book of Prenatal and Postnatal Care.* New York: Howell Book House, 1983.

Holst, Phyllis, DVM. *Canine Reproduction.* Loveland, Colo.: Alpine Publications, 1985.

Walkowicz, Chris and Bonnie Wilcox, DVM. *Successful Dog Breeding, The Complete Handbook of Canine Midwifery.* New York: Howell Book House, 1994.

ABOUT ACTIVITIES

American Rescue Dog Association. *Search and Rescue Dogs.* New York: Howell Book House, 1991.

Barwig, Susan and Stewart Hilliard. *Schutzhund.* New York: Howell Book House, 1991.

Beaman, Arthur S. *Lure Coursing.* New York: Howell Book House, 1994.

Daniels, Julie. *Enjoying Dog Agility—From Backyard to Competition.* New York: Doral Publishing, 1990.

Davis, Kathy Diamond. *Therapy Dogs.* New York: Howell Book House, 1992.

Gallup, Davis Anne. *Running With Man's Best Friend.* Loveland, Colo.: Alpine Publications, 1986.

Habgood, Dawn and Robert. *On the Road Again With Man's Best Friend.* New England, Mid-Atlantic, West Coast and Southeast editions. Selective guides to area bed and breakfasts, inns, hotels and resorts that welcome guests and their dogs. New York: Howell Book House, 1995.

Holland, Vergil S. *Herding Dogs.* New York: Howell Book House, 1994.

LaBelle, Charlene G. *Backpacking With Your Dog.* Loveland, Colo.: Alpine Publications, 1993.

Simmons-Moake, Jane. *Agility Training, The Fun Sport for All Dogs.* New York: Howell Book House, 1991.

Spencer, James B. *Hup! Training Flushing Spaniels the American Way.* New York: Howell Book House, 1992.

Spencer, James B. *Point! Training the All-Seasons Birddog.* New York: Howell Book House, 1995.

Tarrant, Bill. *Training the Hunting Retriever.* New York: Howell Book House, 1991.

Volhard, Jack and Wendy. *The Canine Good Citizen.* New York: Howell Book House, 1994.

General Titles

Haggerty, Captain Arthur J. *How to Get Your Pet Into Show Business.* New York: Howell Book House, 1994.

McLennan, Bardi. *Dogs and Kids, Parenting Tips.* New York: Howell Book House, 1993.

Moran, Patti J. *Pet Sitting for Profit, A Complete Manual for Professional Success.* New York: Howell Book House, 1992.

Scalisi, Danny and Libby Moses. *When Rover Just Won't Do, Over 2,000 Suggestions for Naming Your Dog.* New York: Howell Book House, 1993.

Sife, Wallace, PhD. *The Loss of a Pet.* New York: Howell Book House, 1993.

Wrede, Barbara J. *Civilizing Your Puppy.* Hauppauge, N.Y.: Barron's Educational Series, 1992.

Magazines

The AKC GAZETTE, The Official Journal for the Sport of Purebred Dogs. American Kennel Club, 51 Madison Ave., New York, NY.

Bloodlines Journal. United Kennel Club, 100 E. Kilgore Rd., Kalamazoo, MI.

Dog Fancy. Fancy Publications, 3 Burroughs, Irvine, CA 92718

Dog World. Maclean Hunter Publishing Corp., 29 N. Wacker Dr., Chicago, IL 60606.

Videos

"SIRIUS Puppy Training," by Ian Dunbar, PhD, MRCVS. James & Kenneth Publishers, 2140 Shattuck Ave. #2406, Berkeley, CA 94704. Order from the publisher.

"Training the Companion Dog," from Dr. Dunbar's British TV Series, James & Kenneth Publishers. (See address above).

The American Kennel Club produces videos on every breed of dog, as well as on hunting tests, field trials and other areas of interest to purebred dog owners. For more information, write to AKC/Video Fulfillment, 5580 Centerview Dr., Suite 200, Raleigh, NC 27606.

chapter 13

Resources

Breed Clubs

Every breed recognized by the American Kennel Club has a national (parent) club. National clubs are a great source of information on your breed. You can get the name of the secretary of the club by contacting:

The American Kennel Club
51 Madison Avenue
New York, NY 10010
(212) 696-8200

There are also numerous all-breed, individual breed, obedience, hunting and other special-interest dog clubs across the country. The American Kennel Club can provide you with a geographical list of clubs to find ones in your area. Contact them at the above address.

Registry Organizations

Registry organizations register purebred dogs. The American Kennel Club is the oldest and largest in this country, and currently recognizes over 130 breeds. The United Kennel Club registers some breeds the AKC doesn't (including the American Pit Bull Terrier and the Miniature Fox Terrier) as well as many of the same breeds. The others included here are for your reference; the AKC can provide you with a list of foreign registries.

American Kennel Club
51 Madison Avenue
New York, NY 10010

United Kennel Club (UKC)
100 E. Kilgore Road
Kalamazoo, MI 49001-5598

American Dog Breeders Assn.
P.O. Box 1771
Salt Lake City, UT 84110
(Registers American Pit Bull Terriers)

Canadian Kennel Club
89 Skyway Avenue
Etobicoke, Ontario
Canada M9W 6R4

National Stock Dog Registry
P.O. Box 402
Butler, IN 46721
(Registers working stock dogs)

Orthopedic Foundation for Animals (OFA)
2300 E. Nifong Blvd.
Columbia, MO 65201-3856
(Hip registry)

Activity Clubs

Write to these organizations for information on the
activities they sponsor.

American Kennel Club
51 Madison Avenue
New York, NY 10010
(Conformation Shows, Obedience Trials, Field
Trials and Hunting Tests, Agility, Canine Good

Citizen, Lure Coursing, Herding, Tracking, Earthdog Tests, Coonhunting.)

United Kennel Club
100 E. Kilgore Road
Kalamazoo, MI 49001-5598
(Conformation Shows, Obedience Trials, Agility, Hunting for Various Breeds, Terrier Trials and more.)

North American Flyball Assn.
1342 Jeff St.
Ypsilanti, MI 48198

International Sled Dog Racing Assn.
P.O. Box 446
Norman, ID 83848-0446

North American Working Dog Assn., Inc.
Southeast Kreisgruppe
P.O. Box 833
Brunswick, GA 31521

Trainers

Association of Pet Dog Trainers
P.O. Box 385
Davis, CA 95617
(800) PET–DOGS

American Dog Trainers' Network
161 West 4th St.
New York, NY 10014
(212) 727–7257

National Association of Dog Obedience Instructors
2286 East Steel Rd.
St. Johns, MI 48879

Associations

American Dog Owners Assn.
1654 Columbia Tpk.
Castleton, NY 12033
(Combats anti-dog legislation)

Delta Society
P.O. Box 1080
Renton, WA 98057-1080
(Promotes the human/animal bond through
pet-assisted therapy and other programs)

Dog Writers Assn. of America (DWAA)
Sally Cooper, Secy.
222 Woodchuck Ln.
Harwinton, CT 06791

National Assn. for Search and Rescue (NASAR)
P.O. Box 3709
Fairfax, VA 22038

Therapy Dogs International
6 Hilltop Road
Mendham, NJ 07945